THE GIFT

Also by Shelley Shepard Gray

SISTERS OF THE HEART SERIES
Hidden • *Wanted* • *Forgiven* • *Grace*

SEASONS OF SUGARCREEK SERIES
Winter's Awakening • *Spring's Renewal*
Autumn's Promise • *Christmas in Sugarcreek*

FAMILIES OF HONOR SERIES
The Caregiver • *The Protector* • *The Survivor*
A Christmas for Katie (novella)

THE SECRETS OF CRITTENDEN COUNTY SERIES
Missing • *The Search* • *Found* • *Peace*

THE DAYS OF REDEMPTION SERIES
Daybreak • *Ray of Light* • *Eventide* • *Snowfall*

RETURN TO SUGARCREEK SERIES
Hopeful • *Thankful* • *Joyful*

AMISH BRIDES OF PINECRAFT SERIES
The Promise of Palm Grove
The Proposal at Siesta Key
A Wedding at the Orange Blossom Inn
A Wish on Gardenia Street (novella)
A Christmas Bride in Pinecraft

THE CHARMED AMISH LIFE SERIES
A Son's Vow • *A Daughter's Dream*
A Sister's Wish • *An Amish Family Christmas*

THE AMISH OF HART COUNTY SERIES
Her Secret • *His Guilt*

THE GIFT

THE AMISH OF HART COUNTY

Shelley Shepard Gray

AVON
INSPIRE
An Imprint of HarperCollinsPublishers

This is a work of fiction. Names, characters, places, and incidents are products of the author's imagination or are used fictitiously and are not to be construed as real. Any resemblance to actual events, locales, organizations, or persons, living or dead, is entirely coincidental.

P.S.™ is a trademark of HarperCollins Publishers.

HarperCollins books may be purchased for educational, business, or sales promotional use. For information, please email the Special Markets Department at SPsales@harpercollins.com.

FIRST EDITION

Designed by Diahann Sturge

Library of Congress Cataloging-in-Publication Data has been applied for.

ISBN 978-0-06-246914-4 (paperback)
ISBN 978-0-06-269785-1 (library edition)

17 18 19 20 21   LSC   10 9 8 7 6 5 4 3 2 1

To Dan and Suzanne. With love and friendship, and the hope
that we'll share many more holidays together in the future!

The author is grateful for being allowed to reprint
recipes from Our Family's Favorite Recipes
The Shrock's Homestead
9943 Copperhead Rd. N.W.
Sugarcreek, OH 44681

We walk by faith, not by sight.

2 CORINTHIANS 5:7

Enjoy today. It won't come back.

AMISH PROVERB

CHAPTER 1

*C*rack!
Susanna Schwartz jolted. She knew of only one thing that could make a sound like that. A rifle. Someone was shooting nearby. Right by where she was driving her buggy on Highway 218.

Crack! Ping! Ping!

That sounded closer. She glanced nervously toward the woods but didn't see anything . . . or anyone. Of course, the way the icy snow was falling, it was a wonder she could even see her horse, Star.

She exhaled, tried to calm herself down and concentrate on driving her buggy home. Tried to make some sense of what she was hearing. It was Thanksgiving weekend, the first weekend of the hunting season. At least, it was back in Ohio. Maybe a hunter hadn't realized that he was hunting so close to the road. That had happened all the time in Berlin, where she'd lived until two weeks ago. Boys and men would get so excited about tracking their turkeys and deer, they would neglect to pay attention to their surroundings.

Another crack sounded, just as she was sure a patch of asphalt kicked up. But maybe she'd imagined that?

Exhaling a ragged breath, she attempted to calm her beating heart. No good would come of her getting in a tizzy. If she did that, she'd upset the horse, and then she'd really be in trouble.

But when yet another crack reverberated in the air, fear took over. Star whinnied and attempted to pick up speed.

"Steady, Star," she called out. "Easy, girl. It'll be all right."

At least, she hoped it would. At the moment, she wasn't so sure about that. Everything about her decision to drop off her little sister, Traci, at her girlfriend's house just a few miles from their new farm had been a bad idea.

The snow had already picked up, covering the empty highway in a thick blanket, which had made driving her buggy difficult. The metal wheels had slipped and slid several times since she'd begun the journey.

Now she just wished it hadn't gotten so dark so fast, and so icy. And she really wished the gunshots would stop.

Don't make things worse by imagining things, she cautioned herself. *Focus on what is happening now, not what could be.*

She didn't need to borrow trouble. She needed to do whatever it took to get home as quickly and safely as possible. That meant she needed to remain calm and keep Star's lines firm and steady.

When Star whinnied again, jerking her head to the right, Susanna tightened her grip on the leather straps. "Easy now, Star," she called out once more, hoping and praying that the taut lines and her voice would soothe the mare before she lost control.

But it was too late. Star neighed in alarm and jerked to the right, neighing even more loudly. Then, as another crack reverberated through the air, the horse broke into a gallop.

Heart racing, Susanna leaned forward, holding on to the bench seat with one hand while trying to retain her grip with the other. "*Whoa*, Star! *Please*, Star!"

Her cry did no good.

The buggy wobbled, the wheels sliding precariously on the snow- and ice-covered black asphalt.

The muscles in her arms strained as she attempted to gain control. A steady burn raced up her forearms and biceps as she pulled the reins.

Star scrambled, her horseshoes clattering on the ice and snow. *Ping!*

That was too close. Fully terrorized now, Star was kicking her legs. The action forced one of the lines to the buggy to snap. Seconds felt like minutes as the buggy jerked and slid. When the other line snapped, Star darted forward to safety.

Susanna cried out. Screamed as the buggy slid and rocked precariously. Grasping the seat as tightly as she could, she pressed herself against the side of the closed space. Bracing herself for impact.

Suddenly free, the buggy skidded toward the center of the road.

She grabbed the brake. Attempted to pull. But she might as well have been clutching air. The buggy spun, then slid toward the other side, racing toward the ditch.

She was going to crash. Desperately, she tried to focus on

where she was. But between the frost on the windshield and the sleet and ice falling in thick sheets from the sky, there was no way to tell.

All she knew for sure was that she was stranded on an unfamiliar road in the middle of an ice storm. And someone was shooting a rifle nearby.

Crying now, she closed her eyes, held on to whatever she could, and prayed.

Prayed as hard as she could. Prayed like she never had before.

And as the conveyance fell down into the ditch, crashing into a thicket of trees, the force of the impact threw her toward the door. It flew open and she was thrown out, landing on her side, her arms barely bracing her. Her body twisted and useless.

She'd gotten out. She'd survived.

But as the snow and ice fell against her skin, stinging like sharp pellets, Susanna wondered if that was enough. Then she didn't care at all as she slipped into unconsciousness.

"*JAH.* THERE YOU go," a soft masculine voice whispered by her side. "Come now, give it a try again. Open your eyes."

Susanna willed herself to try to do as the soothing voice bade. But it felt impossible. Her head was pounding and each of her eyelids felt like it weighed a hundred pounds. Then, too, her skin felt cold. So cold. Freezing. Unable to help herself, she moaned.

A warm hand glided across her cheek. It paused, then ran across her brow. The motion was soothing. Almost reassuring. "Ach. I know it's hard, girl. But give it another go. *Jah?*"

She tried again. This time, she was able to open her eyes a

little. She saw it was still dark out, but there was a flickering light nearby, and the low beam of a flashlight on the ground. The beam reflected the white from the snow, making the area seem brighter . . . and vaguely foreign.

She blinked to focus. Then stared into the light-blue eyes of her rescuer.

"Look at that. They're green." He smiled, revealing a slightly crooked incisor.

Green? Blinking again, Susanna gasped as she attempted to find her voice.

"*Nee.* Don't talk. There's no need for that," he murmured, pulling back enough for her to see more of his features. His wide brow. The line of his jaw. The chunk of dark-brown hair mixing in with dark, thick eyebrows. "A car stopped just up ahead. My friend Lora just happened to be the driver. She's callin' for an ambulance. You should stay still until they come."

His words didn't make a bit of sense. Until she remembered what had just happened.

Panic engulfed her. "Star?"

Where was she? The buggy? Her horse? Had Star been hurt? Was she somewhere nearby, cut or injured?

"Star?" He turned a puzzled eye to the heavens.

Unable to do anything else, she, too, looked above.

"*Nee*, I don't see no stars out. 'Course, it's a bad night out here. Ain't so? Sleeting and spitting snow. Miserable weather for Thanksgiving." Kneeling closer, he smoothed the blanket over her. "Good thing I had this. We need to keep you warm."

His words, though he had completely misunderstood her, reminded her of where she was. It was Friday night, the evening after Thanksgiving. She'd been driving back from dropping Traci off at a new friend's house. She'd gotten a late start back because they'd invited her inside for a slice of pumpkin pie.

While she'd been inside, the wind had changed direction. That change had turned the lightly falling snow into hard pellets of deadly ice. Right about that time, darkness had fallen, enveloping her and Star in a thick, soupy world. She'd had to slow Star's pace so her hooves wouldn't slip on the asphalt.

Then those shots were fired.

"Shots?" she blurted. Her voice sounded hoarse and distorted, even to her own ears.

He frowned. "I reckon you will have to get some shots, but maybe not." When she parted her lips, desperate to make him understand, he started talking again. "You'll be all right in no time," he said with a reassuring smile. "Don't doubt that. Good enough to start your Christmas baking . . . Ah, here's Lora. Let me see what she says."

He stood up abruptly, shaking off one of his boots. "Did you get hold of your husband?"

"I did," the English woman said, her voice drifting slowly toward Susanna. "And thank the good Lord I did, too. Eddie was so worried when he'd tried my cell phone a couple of minutes ago and I didn't answer. Anyway, I told him about the accident. He dispatched an ambulance from the radio in his car. He should be here any second, too." Lowering her voice, she whispered, "How's she doing?"

"Don't know. She seems fairly sluggish."

"She probably has a concussion."

"*Jah*. I thought that, too. She's talking and her pretty green eyes are open. So, that's *gut*. Right?"

"I think so. So, who is she? Do you know? Has she said anything about what happened?"

"I ain't been having much of a conversation, Lora. She ain't making much sense anyway. She's asking about stars and shots. I haven't even gotten to introductions yet."

The woman's chuckle echoed through the air. "Honestly. The things you say."

"Hey, now . . ."

"You know I'm only having a bit of fun with you."

"At my expense . . ."

"Go on, now. You wait for Eddie. I'll join her. Poor thing, lying alone on the shoulder of the pavement." Smiling softly, she stepped closer, then knelt down on the ground beside Susanna. "Hi, there. I'm Lora Beck," she said softly.

"Hi," Susanna replied, taking in the attractive woman's golden hair falling past her shoulders, her brown eyes, green turtleneck, jeans, and puffy down coat.

"My husband is a cop. Well, a sheriff. Well, a sheriff's deputy," she amended, her tone easy and light. She paused before gently wiping Susanna's face with a soft cloth again. "Anyways, he's on his way. So's an ambulance. I know you're cold and hurting, but hold on a little longer, okay?"

It took effort, but Susanna answered. "'Kay."

"If you're talking, that's a good thing." Leaning closer, Lora smiled. "That Neil is so silly. He was acting like you don't know what's going on, but you're gonna be all right, aren't you? I bet you're going to be just fine."

Before Susanna could attempt to answer that, the sound of

sirens lit the air. Help was on the way. Thank the good Lord for that!

Closing her eyes, she allowed her mind to relax. At the moment, it didn't really matter where this man, this Neil, had come from, did it? Or why shots had been fired.

Only that she'd survived.

There would be time enough to figure out who everyone was and how they came to be near her when her head wasn't pounding, her body didn't feel beaten, and she wasn't freezing cold, lying on the hard pavement.

At least, she hoped and prayed that was so.

CHAPTER 2

I'm so glad you are nice," a sweet-looking blond woman about ten years older than Susanna said as they joined the buffet line after the three-hour-long church service. "I didn't think you would be."

As the statement registered, Susanna felt her smile falter.

She should have been used to comments like this by now. Ever since she and her family moved here almost a month ago, all the adults in the community seemed to have a grudge against them. Try as they might, no one in her family could figure out exactly why.

Though her sister Amanda was sending her a warning look, Susanna realized she was more than a little tired of being in the dark.

Maybe it was time to get some answers. "I'm sorry if I've done something to offend you," she replied in as conciliatory a tone as she was able. "If you tell me what I've done, I'll attempt to make things better."

The woman looked taken aback. "You haven't done anything."

"No?"

"*Nee.* I mean, not besides the obvious."

"I'm sorry, but I'm still not following you."

The blonde flushed. "You know . . . the way you treated the Vance family."

"Me?"

She waved a hand. "I suppose it was your parents. The way they were so heavy-handed when they purchased the Vances' farm."

Now she was even more confused. "My family bought the Vances' farm after they put it up for sale. There isn't much more to the story than that."

"Of course there is."

"I'm afraid I don't understand. What was wrong with someone wanting to buy a farm that was up for sale?"

"Don't make it sound like you are the innocent party. You and your family took advantage of the Vances' difficult situation."

"What situation?"

"I'm certainly not going to discuss it here with you."

But hadn't *she* just brought it up? Even more confused, Susanna glanced at her sister. Amanda was younger, but only by a year. She also had a better sense of handling difficult people.

But Amanda looked as perplexed as she felt.

Susanna was no expert on buying or selling real estate, but it sure seemed like far too many people were not only interested in their private business, but had a lot of emotional feelings about it, too.

And that didn't make any sense.

Since she couldn't think of a way to get better information without sounding like she was picking a fight, Susanna decided a slight change of subject might be in order. "I'm so glad we finally got to go to church today. I was home on bed rest for so long, I was getting a bit stir crazy."

The woman flushed. "Of course. I heard about your buggy accident. It must have been so scary."

"It was. It was one of the scariest things I've ever been through." Right up there with sitting in a hospital waiting room while her mother had emergency surgery.

"It's a blessing you weren't badly hurt."

"I agree." Physically, she was better. Mentally? Well, that was another story. Almost nightly, she'd wake up in a cold sweat, reliving the sound of gunshots. Of Star panicking and the buggy sliding out of control . . .

When she'd woken up in the hospital, her mother was sitting by her side. Mamm's face was stark white. The only color Susanna saw came from her blue eyes—she'd been crying for hours.

Susanna had sustained a concussion, a colorful array of bumps and bruises, and some really awful scrapes on her arms and hands. But miraculously, nothing had been broken.

It truly was a blessing.

The doctors had kept her another day, then sent her home with firm warnings about taking things easy.

That hadn't been hard to agree to. She'd felt as if . . . well, as if she'd been thrown from a moving buggy. Every part of her body ached.

Then, too, there was the grief she felt for Star. Star's leg had been injured in her frantic bolt. The sheriff who came out to the scene of the accident had to put her down, right on the side of the road. Though Susanna knew she couldn't have done anything differently, the loss of Star hit her hard. They'd had her for years, and she was such a steady, sweet-natured horse. Susanna felt like she'd let Star down. Almost as difficult to bear was the knowledge that her father was now going to have to buy another horse and buggy. It was a costly expense she knew they couldn't really afford. Not after they'd used the majority of their savings to purchase the farm.

Days after Susanna had returned home, she caught a terrible cold. She was so feverish and sick, her family hadn't even gone to church.

Now, here it was, a little over two weeks later, and they came to church only to discover that while some people were cordial, others, like this woman in line, were far more standoffish.

Disappointment coursed through her. She'd been so excited to finally make friends, but it had become evident that even the Christmas holiday wasn't inspiring many of her neighbors to become more cordial.

As she scooped a small amount of pasta salad onto her plate, Susanna decided to stop worrying about things. Of course it was going to take time to make friends! She was simply being sensitive.

"I heard that you thought someone shot at you," a dark-haired woman on the other side of the blonde said.

Maybe she wasn't being sensitive after all. "I didn't *imagine* I heard gunshots. I *know* I did. Someone was firing a rifle in the dark."

"How can you be sure?" she asked. "Did they find any casings?"

"Not that I'm aware of."

"Your buggy wasn't actually hit, was it?"

"*Nee*. But the gunfire scared my horse."

"Shame, that."

"*Jah*." Actually, so much about their move to Kentucky had been a disappointment.

"Though our first weeks here have been eventful, I'm looking forward to celebrating Christmas here in Kentucky," Amanda said, in that friendly way of hers that she'd mastered around the age of four. "Hart County is so different, but I'm sure we'll enjoy the holidays very much."

The woman's posture eased. "I'm glad you are settling in. Now that you all are getting out and about, I suppose we'll get to know each other better."

"I imagine we will," Amanda said with an angelic smile. It was another move she'd mastered.

Amanda was born with golden-blond hair and cornflower-blue eyes. She *was* bright, while Susanna appeared, with her brown hair and hazel eyes, more burnished. Amanda's personality matched her appearance. She was vivacious and chatty while Susanna often struggled to find the right words to say.

"Would you girls like to sit with us?" the blond woman asked. "My name's Rachel, by the way."

"We would. *Danke*, Rachel," Amanda said eagerly.

"But of course. We want to do everything we can to help ease your transition here." Smiling far more warmly at Amanda, Rachel gestured to one of the long tables near the end of the driveway. "I'll save you both a seat. You are okay eating outside, aren't you? It's a little chilly, but since the sun is out today, it's better than being in the barn. It can get stuffy in there."

"Oh, I agree," Amanda said with an even brighter smile. "Now that most of the snow has melted, eating outside in the fresh air is *wunderbaar*. Before we know it, we'll all be stuck inside for weeks."

"*Jah*," Susanna agreed. When Rachel and Amanda both turned to her, obviously hoping to hear something interesting or cute, she only smiled awkwardly. "It's good to appreciate nice days, the weather is so unpredictable." Of course, she realized that she was talking about so much more than the weather.

As they followed the other women out of the barn and over to a long table situated in the sun, Susanna scanned the crowd, especially the group of young men sitting near to where the food was set up. "Hey, Amanda? Do you see any man who looks the way I described my hero?" The paramedics had told her that the man who had rescued her asked not to be identified.

She'd thought that odd. Her father had, too. But her mother pointed out that the man might be afraid that they would do something to embarrass him. Some people didn't like to be thanked.

Susanna had been really hoping to catch sight of him. Before church, when all the young people were milling around, she'd scanned the area carefully. But so far, no one looked like that burly man with the pale-blue eyes and ruddy complexion.

Amanda shook her head. "It's too bad you don't remember more details about your mystery man's appearance."

"I had a concussion and it was pitch-black outside. I was otherwise occupied," she said with a grin. "I did remember his light-colored eyes, though. I know I would remember them. They were so light, one might even think they were gray."

"Maybe we can ask Rachel and her friends if they have any idea who the man is."

"That's a *gut* idea."

When they joined Rachel, the rest of the seats at the table were filled. After smiling at everyone, Susanna took a bite of her chicken and concentrated on learning more about the ladies.

First, there was Ava and her two daughters, Rachel and Ruth; then, there was Charity, the woman in line with dark hair, and sitting near her was her sister, Camilla. At the end of the table was Maggie, who didn't say much but seemed to listen and watch all of them intently.

"Are you enjoying your new home?" Charity asked.

Susanna barely stifled a sigh. She had hoped to not talk about their house anymore, since it seemed to bring up so many bad feelings.

She studied Charity closely. Why had she brought it up? Was she being snide . . . or was it merely Susanna's imagination? Shaking off the sense of unease, she nodded. "We are. It's plenty big and has two bathrooms, which is always good when there are three girls in the house," she joked.

If she had known them better, she would have explained how, compared to the small duplex they'd lived in back in Berlin, the purchase of this farm in Kentucky was a dream come true for all of them.

From the time she'd been a child, Susanna had hardly seen her father. In order to support them, he'd managed a wealthy Englisher's farm. Because of the distance away, he'd even slept in a small suite of rooms in the back of one of his barns four or five nights a week.

While he was working, their mother took care of her,

Amanda, and their little sister, Traci. Susanna knew her mother was lonely, and they all missed their happy, hard-working, affectionate father. But she'd also learned not to complain or wish for anything different. They were blessed to have each other.

But then about a year ago, two things happened that changed everything. First, their mother contracted a series of illnesses, eventually being in bed for almost a month with pneumonia. Their father worried about her terribly.

The second thing had been even harder on their father. The gentleman he worked for passed away—and had gifted him in his will with a sizable amount of money. Enough money for Daed to buy a farm of his own.

That money, combined with the money he'd saved, had been an answer to a prayer . . . until he realized how very little it would buy in Holmes County, Ohio. The land there was expensive. That's when he hired a real estate agent and started searching for another location.

Which brought them to Kentucky and to the Vances' property.

All that was why she hated to apologize for her father being so tough in his negotiations for that farm. If it had been more expensive, they would still be in their duplex, waiting to find the perfect piece of land for them.

But it sure didn't seem like anyone here was interested in hearing their side of the sale. As the minutes wore on, everyone looked increasingly uncomfortable.

"What, um, Susanna means to say is that we are sure we will be mighty happy here," Amanda said, for once sounding as tentative as her sister. "We feel blessed that the house came up for sale when it did."

But if anything, the mention of being blessed seemed to bother everyone even more. Rachel exchanged glances with her girlfriends.

Sipping her coffee, Susanna was starting to wish they'd simply gone home right after church. She'd much rather be sitting in their family room reading than navigating her way through this awkward conversation.

Deciding to finish as quickly as possible, she took a big bite of macaroni.

Obviously resolving to smooth things over, Amanda smiled at everyone. "Can any of you all do us a favor? You see, when Susanna got in the accident, a local man came to her rescue. We know what he looks like but not his name."

"That's intriguing. Was he Amish?"

Susanna nodded. "He was. He was so kind, too. I kept hoping that he would stop by our house and say hello, but that hasn't happened." She shrugged. "But maybe he didn't know my name, either."

"That's probably true. There are a lot of Amish in the county, now. It ain't like it used to be, when we all knew each other and our horses, too."

Susanna began to relax. Maybe this was going to be all right. She just had to stop from taking offense at every imagined slight.

"Describe him the best you can. Then I'll start bringing likely men over," Charity said with a smirk.

Susanna could just imagine how awkward that would be! "*Nee,*" she said quickly. "There's no need for that."

"Come on. It will be fun. What's the benefit of sitting with people who know everyone if you don't put us to good use?"

Amanda grinned. "She has a point, Sue."

"All right. You're right." Smiling awkwardly, she said, "Well, the man was large."

"Fat?"

"Oh, *nee*. He was built large, but not fat. More like a football player. Tall, too."

"What color were his hair and eyes?"

"He had on a knit cap, but his eyebrows looked kind of brown."

"Dark or light brown?"

She had to think for a minute. "Dark brown. I think."

"And his eyes?"

"That, I remember," she said with a smile, pleased at the game. "Light blue." Remembering something else, she said, "Oh, and he had fair skin."

"So you were rescued by a tall, hefty man with light-brown hair, fair skin, and light-blue eyes."

"*Jah*. He had a deep voice, too. Kind of scratchy, but I could be wrong about that."

She felt a new kind of tension as the other women exchanged glances. "What? Any ideas?"

Charity nodded. Rachel looked pained.

"What did I say?" Susanna asked. "Is something wrong?"

Again, everyone looked awkwardly at each other.

"You all are starting to make me worried," Amanda joked. "What is the matter?"

"Nothing, except the man you are describing sounds an awful lot like"—Charity looked around, then pointed to a trio of men standing by the barn—"him."

"Who?" Susanna got to her feet and turned. Staring at the men.

Just then, one of them looked directly at her. His gaze was

solemn and blue. His pale cheeks were scruffy. He had on a thick wool coat, but even in the company of other men who were bundled up, he stood out.

He blinked, as he obviously recognized her, too.

She smiled.

Oh, but this was wonderful! At last, she was going to be able to thank him in person.

"Susanna, sit down," Amanda said.

"I can't. That's him," she said as she was about to begin walking his way. "Ladies, thank you! I've been so worried I wasn't going to be able to thank him properly."

Just then she noticed that the other women still weren't smiling. "What?" she whispered. "What is wrong?"

"You really don't know who he is, do you?" Rachel asked at last.

"I know he saved my life. What's his name?"

"That is Neil Vance."

"Neil *Vance*?"

As if reading her mind, Rachel nodded. "That very one. Your family bought his family's farm."

She felt like every bit of food she'd just consumed was now lodged in her windpipe. "That is quite a coincidence."

"It's something, all right. Because your parents didn't want to pay a fair price for the farm, they are all living in a relative's tiny older house. Everyone is struggling to make ends meet. At Christmastime, no less."

"Instead of a coincidence, I think we should call it ironic. That's more fitting. Ain't so?" Charity asked the table at large.

Now Amanda was finally getting angry. "What is ironic?"

"Well, Neil Vance saved Susanna's life, just days after all of you practically ruined his."

CHAPTER 3

Sunday, December 10

"Well, I'll be," Neil Vance muttered as he watched the brown-haired woman with the striking green eyes approach. There she was, just as if she'd stepped out of a dream.

Or at least a mighty good memory.

"Who's that?" Dale Kaufmann, his best friend and former neighbor, asked as he caught sight of the woman approaching him.

"That is the girl I saved in that buggy accident in November." Unable to help himself, he smiled. Looked like some wishes did actually come true.

Dale pulled the brim of his black hat down over his eyes so he could stare at her without looking too rude. "You didn't tell me she was so pretty."

"I thought she had pleasing features, but I didn't remember her being so pretty."

"What? Were you blind?"

Turning away, Neil tossed Dale a disparaging look. "It was pitch-black. And snowing. Plus, she was on the ground and hurt. I wasn't exactly checking her out. I was helping her, you know."

"I would have helped her, too, of course." He paused. "But then I would have noticed what she looked like."

"Somehow, I think you would have." Dale had always been a flirt.

"Don't act like I'm being rude. You're noticing now." He smirked. "If you ain't careful, she's going to realize you're staring at her as much as I am."

"Shut up and be nice," Neil hissed under his breath as he stepped forward. "Hi."

"Hi." Looking from him to Dale and then back again, the woman flushed. "I'm sorry to interrupt your conversation."

"It weren't important," Dale quipped.

She smiled, then looked back at Neil. "This is kinda awkward. I mean, I don't know if you remember me—"

He smiled. "I remember you." When she still looked unsure, he added, "You made a pretty big impression on me, seeing as how I was worried that you were gonna die." As Dale jabbed him in the ribs with his elbow, he realized that was pretty blunt. "Sorry. I mean, I don't think I could forget about you if I tried."

Her green eyes warmed, making them look almost liquid. "You did save my life. I'd venture to say it ain't every day that a man gets to be such a hero."

"I'm glad I happened to be there. I guess the Lord intended for me to be taking a walk that Friday night."

But instead of looking relieved, something in his words made her look even more fretful. "I have wondered why you were there . . . we seemed to be the only two people in the area."

He wasn't sure, but he kind of thought he heard a layer of

doubt in her tone. "Obviously, that wasn't the case. Someone was shooting that rifle and it wasn't me or you."

"Oh! Yes. Of course. It's a blessing you happened to be nearby. An answer to a prayer, for sure." Before he could comment on that, she continued. "Anyway, I remembered you, too, though I didn't catch your name."

"It's—"

Looking increasingly troubled, she talked right over him, continuing in a rush. "I'm Susanna. I had thought maybe the deputy would have told me your name when he came by the hospital, but he didn't. So I never got the chance to ask him who you were. If I would have known, I would have thanked you before now."

"No thanks are necessary," he said, meaning every word. "I'm just glad I was there to help you. But let's fix our introductions now, okay? I'm Neil Vance. And this is my friend Dale Kaufmann."

"It's nice to meet you, Susanna," Dale said. "Mighty nice."

As usual, Dale was putting on his charm a bit too thickly. Feeling a little possessive over her, though that made no sense, Neil said, "Don't mind Dale. He's just overtly friendly. Like a, um, puppy or something."

Dale raised his brows. "Really, Neil?"

"Weren't you just telling me that you needed to leave?"

"I was not." Turning to Susanna, Dale said, "Since you are new, we noticed you from across the yard. Where did you move here from?"

"Funny you should ask that." She cleared her throat as she awkwardly gestured over to a table of women watching their interplay. "I came from Ohio. I mean, my family did. And, um, I was just telling those ladies that I remembered what my rescuer looked like, but I hadn't caught your name. After I described you, they pointed you out. I canna hardly believe it."

"Small world, right?"

"*Jah.*" Her smile eased slightly, but it was still tremulous. Neil wondered why. Was she naturally shy? Did she think he was going to get mad at her or something because she sought him out? If so, he needed to fix that.

Stepping closer, he smiled as he folded his hands behind his back. "I'm glad you came over to say hello. I've thought about that night more than once. I wondered what happened to you. You okay now?"

She nodded. "I'm fine. Neil, I just want to say . . . well, I just want you to know that I'm so very grateful to you. You saved my life that night."

"I don't know if I did that, but I'm glad I was there to help you."

"*Nee*, I'm fairly certain you did. The *doktah* at the hospital told me that my Good Samaritan gave me a wonderful early Christmas gift. You gave me my life."

"You're embarrassing me now," he teased.

She laughed. "I'll stop, then. Embarrassing you wouldn't be the way I'd ever want to repay you."

When she laughed, Neil thought her face fairly glowed. Barely able to stop staring, he looked down at his boots as he sought to regain his composure.

He wasn't sure why God had meant for the two of them to have crossed paths that way, but now he was thinking that surely the Lord had intended for them to know each other well. For what other reason could He have given them such an incredible meeting?

He had to see her again.

"Listen, where are you living? Maybe I could stop by one evening this week after work."

"I would like that, but, um, well, after the girls told me your name, I realized something else. Something that you might not know about me."

"And what is that?" He could only imagine what tales those girls had told her.

"Um, well, you see, my full name is Susanna Schwartz."

"Schwartz." He'd literally choked out the name.

While Susanna continued to stand there motionless, obviously waiting for him to absolve her of any guilt she might be feeling, Neil felt every muscle in his shoulders and neck tense.

Actually, he felt like he was cracking into a dozen pieces. Though of course she had nothing to do with his father's poor financial investments, his secrets, or his increasingly outlandish ways of solving their problems.

But while he knew that, he also knew that this woman who was standing in front of him—looking so composed and, well, perfect—seemed to symbolize everything that had been taken away from him.

Dale stared at her. "You're my neighbor?"

"Well, ah . . . I guess I am. I mean, my family is, if the Vances used to live near you."

"They did," Dale said. "Our farm lies just to the north of yours."

Looking just as perturbed as Neil was feeling, Susanna looked down at the skirt of her forest-green dress before lifting her chin again. "So, Neil, if you want to stop by, you would need to come to your old house."

"I won't be doing that."

"Yes. Well, um, I guess it would feel a bit awkward . . ."

Her voice drifted off. It was obvious that she wasn't sure how to smooth things over.

But that was the problem, wasn't it? There wasn't a way to do that.

"It would be more than a bit awkward, given the way your family forced us out before the holidays."

"I'm sorry, I don't under—"

"My parents asked, practically pleaded, to push the closing to January. But your parents wouldn't budge. For some reason, you had to be in our house before Thanksgiving."

Tears filled her eyes.

"Neil," Dale said under his breath. "Stop."

Seeing her dismay, watching those tears, Neil knew he should stop talking. He was being mean. Worse than that, really.

"I see." The way she was staring at him told him everything he needed to know. She looked guilty.

And though he knew better, a small part of him was glad about that.

By now, she probably had heard that his parents really hadn't wanted to move; that it was only because of his father's poor money management, gambling, and that he owed his uncle Joseph so much.

His *daed* hated owing his brother the way he did, and Neil couldn't really blame him for feeling that way, either. Uncle Joseph was the type of relative to bring up another person's faults at every opportunity. Daed had finally had enough and put the farm on the market—even though Uncle Joseph had simply wanted his father to deed the land to him.

Neil's *mamm* had cried when they put the house up for sale. Things had gotten worse when months passed and there were no takers. Against the real estate agent's advice, they kept dropping the price. Then dropped it some more. And when it was at a rock-bottom price, the Schwartz family swooped in. Then, to everyone's dismay, they'd countered with an even smaller amount. It had been insulting.

But by this time, Uncle Joseph was clamoring to be repaid his money—or for Neil's father to simply give him the farm. But his *daed* said he would rather sell the place to strangers than watch his little brother mismanage what was supposed to be his sons' inheritance.

All of that meant that his parents had made precious little money on the place. After paying the debts, his dad had to further swallow his pride by moving into the small house on the edge of Joseph's property.

"Look, I appreciate you coming over to thank me. That had to have been hard. I think we should agree, though, that we don't have anything to say to each other."

Before she could respond, Dale spoke. "Hey now, Neil. You can't be putting all the blame on Susanna. It ain't her fault."

"Stay out of this, Dale. It ain't none of your business."

Glancing at Susanna again, who was now pale, Dale shook his head. "I can't. I live next door to her now." Softening both his tone and his expression, he said to Susanna, "It's good to meet you. I'll tell my family that you were kind enough to introduce yourself. I'm sure my mother will be by sometime soon."

"*Danke.* I hope that we could maybe one day be friends."

"I hope so, too."

After sharing a tremulous smile with Dale, Susanna visibly steadied herself, then turned to Neil. "I know it must be hard, leaving your land, but it was for sale. My parents only bought it."

"I ain't going to talk about this now."

"So what happened in the storm, you saving me, holding my hand in the snow, it means nothing?"

"I would have done the same for anyone lying on the side of the road. But do I want to know you? Do I want to one day be friends?" he asked, his voice derisive. *"Nee."*

She flinched. "Simply because we're living in your old house?"

"It's because of more than that. A lot more."

Turning his back on her, he walked down the driveway. He sensed that she was still standing there. Probably still staring at him while wearing a look of hurt and confusion.

Their meeting and the way he'd left her would no doubt create a lot of talk among their friends and neighbors. He should care that he'd just publicly embarrassed her. He should be embarrassed about his behavior. This was not who he was.

But right at this moment, he couldn't think of anything beyond that he needed to put some distance between himself and Susanna Schwartz.

The sooner the better.

CHAPTER 4

"Neil?" Dale called. "Hey, Neil. Wait up."

He slowed his pace but didn't stop. He couldn't. He was already so on edge, he feared that if he stood completely still he was going to do something he would regret. He wasn't sure what. Maybe yell at his best friend? Maybe yell at the world?

Seconds later, Dale caught up to his side. "What happened with you back there?"

"You know what happened. I lost my temper."

"I get that. But all Susanna Schwartz wanted was to thank you for helping her. You practically bit her head off."

"No need to start exaggerating. What I did was bad enough."

"Ah. So, you are saying you know what you did. Why did you act like such a jerk, then?" Dale's voice was thick with impatience. "It wasn't her fault that her parents wanted a good deal on their new home."

That hurt. Maybe because everything Dale was saying was true. But what Dale wasn't experiencing was all the pressures Neil had been dealing with at home. He and his brother had jobs now. Every day, they watched their father swallow the last of his pride and work his younger brother's farm. And their mother? She silently did her best to act like everything was fine.

Watching everyone's pain was incredibly difficult.

Having Dale talk to Susanna like they were going to be good neighbors to each other had been the last straw. "I can't talk about this."

Dale gripped his arm. "Sure you can. You must. You need to swallow your pride and go back there and apologize."

"I canna do that right now."

"If not now, when?"

Neil pulled his arm away from Dale's grip. "I don't know, okay? Look, I know I shouldn't have acted that way. I already feel bad about it, too. But I've got no more inside of me for Susanna Schwartz right now. I've got too much else to worry about. I've lost everything."

Dale shook his head slowly. "That's where you are wrong. You still have a lot to be grateful for. You have your parents, your brother, and a place to live. You have a new job. You have your health. You have friends who care about you. You definitely haven't lost everything. Try to remember that, wouldja?"

"See you later, Dale." He turned and picked up his pace, knowing that Dale was right . . . and he was also so wrong.

While it was true that Neil still did have much to be grateful for, everything he'd ever known had been changed. Everything had changed and he was barely able to pick up all the pieces.

HE WALKED FOR another hour. Eventually, a bank of puffy clouds slowly drifted over the horizon, turning the bright day into a far more dreary one. With it, a new chill seeped into his bones. Deciding that no good was going to come from walking and fuming and wishing for things that weren't anymore, he headed home at last.

He wasn't looking forward to it. It was becoming increasingly hard to sit inside his family's very small house on his uncle's farm.

A few days ago, he'd come to the realization that it wasn't just the loss of his home that was so hard. It was the fact that all four of them had seemed determined to dwell on their unhappiness.

Uncle Joseph didn't make things easier. He was his *daed*'s younger brother, and Neil and Roy had often privately thought that he was something of a jerk. Neil couldn't remember a time when his uncle hadn't been in some kind of competition with their father.

Daed used to laugh it off. After Joseph's visits, he'd simply shrug and assure them that his brother couldn't hurt his feelings because the things that he so valued—profits and money—couldn't compare to the many blessings he had.

Mamm had always agreed and teasingly thanked their father by kissing his whiskered cheek.

When he and Roy were younger, Neil had thought that little display of affection was far too sweet and a little embarrassing. After all, he didn't know of any other parents who were so affectionate with each other. But as he'd gotten older, Neil began to understand what his father was saying. Joseph had never married or had children. He had no one to go home to at night or who was waiting for him, excited to share the day's news.

But over the last three years, when the farm began to struggle and their crops didn't fare as well as some of the other
farms in the area, his father's attitude seemed to change.

Little by little, the easygoing, fun-loving man they'd always known had been replaced by someone far different.
Daed started visiting his brother more often.

Only when the farm went up for sale did Neil and Roy
discover the reasons for those visits. Their father had been
borrowing money to make ends meet. Then he'd started
gambling. And he lost even more money.

Though his father never completely came out and said it,
Neil was sure his uncle was lording that over him. That was
why their father had been so ready to sell. He'd hoped to
make enough on the farm to pay back his brother and buy a
smaller farm and begin again.

But they hadn't gotten near what he'd hoped to get for
the land.

Which was why they were now renting the old house on
their uncle's property while Daed helped his brother farm and
Neil and Roy worked at other jobs. Even their mother was
making Christmas cookies, pies, and cakes and selling them
at Bill's Diner or taking orders from friends and neighbors.

One day things would be good again. One day, too, he was
sure he'd stop blaming Susanna and her family for buying
their farm. In his heart, he knew it wasn't their fault.

So, he was definitely going to do that. He was going to
make amends and encourage the rest of the family to do the
same. But just not yet. He reckoned that some things simply
took time to accomplish. This had to be one of them.

Determined to shake off his doldrums, Neil strode past

his uncle's large house and continued on his way to their home at the back of the property. He opened the door, resolved to put a positive spin on the church service for his family. He needed to, if he was going to persuade the other members in the house to once again make church a priority.

But the moment he walked inside, he was overwhelmed with the heavy burden of their circumstances all over again. The interior felt claustrophobic. Stifling. Sure that they would be moving sooner than later, his parents weren't willing to be persuaded to part with any of their furniture or treasures. Because of that, most of the furniture that had occupied their old four-thousand-square-foot house was now crammed into a sixteen-hundred-square-foot space. Neil often felt like a rat in a science experiment, weaving his way around large pieces of furniture in order to get from room to room.

Only his brother and he had given away their furniture. Deciding to use the second bedroom as a space for their dining room set and boxes of extra books and household items, Roy and he had elected to sleep on pallets on the floor in the small living room.

Though it was now almost one in the afternoon, those pallets were still on the floor.

Roy and his mother were sitting on stools in the kitchen, eating turkey sandwiches.

"How was church?" Mamm asked.

"It was fine. There was a nice crowd there. Almost every family was in attendance. You were missed."

"I meant to go, but I got a large order last night from a B&B over in Cub Run." She gestured to the kitchen counters, which were now covered with crescent- and star-shaped cookies.

"They expected you to work on a Sunday?"

"They asked if I would be able to deliver everything to them Monday morning. I said I could." She lifted her chin. "It's good money, son."

"Sorry, Mamm. I didn't mean to sound like that."

"No need to apologize." Looking at Roy, she said, "It hasn't been too bad. Your brother has been helping me."

Neil raised his eyebrows. "Really?"

"I'll have you know that I can cut out star-shaped cookies as well as anyone," he joked.

Neil felt all the tension he'd been holding tight inside him slowly ease. It almost felt like how it used to. Walking to the refrigerator, he pulled out an apple and sat down on the last empty stool. "Where's Daed?"

"Helping Onkle Joseph," Roy said.

"Doing what?" He barely refrained from pointing out that they'd never done more than take care of the animals on Sundays.

Roy shrugged. "Who knows? He's probably making Daed do yet another chore he made up."

"Roy, you mustn't talk that way," Mamm chided.

"Why not? It's true. Uncle Joseph loves to hang his charity over our heads. Worse, he seems to really enjoy watching Daed follow his directives. It's terrible."

"Your words aren't helping to make things better, son."

"They don't make them worse, either."

After taking another bite of her sandwich, Mamm turned to him. "Let's talk about something better now, shall we? Neil, tell me how church was. I hated to miss it. Who did you see? What is new with everyone?"

"Did you see Dale?" Roy asked. "What about Beth?"

Beth was Dale's sister. Roy had been fond of her for years.

Pretty much everyone in both of their families had expected them to be engaged by now. However, things between them seemed to have cooled, and not only because they no longer lived next door to each other.

Roy wouldn't really talk about it, but Neil feared it had a lot to do with their recent financial situation. "I saw Dale but didn't see Beth."

"Why not?" said Roy. "She was there, wasn't she? Or was she home?"

"I didn't see her, but that don't mean much. I didn't get a chance to talk to many people."

"Surely," their *mamm* said, "you weren't rushing to get back here."

It was so rare for their mother to say things like that, Neil almost smiled. "You are right. I wasn't in a hurry to rest among all this furniture." Bracing himself, he broke his news. "The truth is that I met Susanna Schwartz."

Mamm blinked. "Who?"

Roy's expression darkened. "She's one of the daughters who moved into our old farm." Raising his eyebrows at him, Roy inserted a new, darker tone into his voice. "Ain't that right?"

"It is. The Schwartzes have three daughters," Neil said.

"Oh. Oh, yes. I should have remembered that. My stars. I bet Mrs. Schwartz has her hands full with three girls." Looking ill at ease, she stood up. After washing her hands, she pulled out a large metal rectangular tin and started layering cookies and waxed paper inside. "What is she like?" she asked.

The question was innocuous, but her voice sounded strained.

Neil, ignoring Roy's glare for upsetting their mother, tried to describe Susanna as best he could. "She has dark hair and green eyes. She's slim, too."

"Is she pretty?"

"*Jah.*" Actually, at first, he'd thought she was very pretty. Thinking there was no way to ease into it, he added, "It turns out that she and I had already met. She's the woman I helped that night after Thanksgiving."

Both Roy and his mother gaped at him. "Isn't that something?" his mother murmured.

"What did she have to say?" Roy asked.

Feeling his face flush, Neil said, "She sought me out to thank me. She said she had never caught my name, which was why she hadn't thanked me before now."

"That is considerate of her. At least she's a nice woman. That gives me some comfort. So, are they settling in all right?"

His mother's graciousness shamed him. "I'm afraid I didn't ask."

"Oh? Why not?"

He sighed. "Speaking to Susanna was awkward."

"I bet," Roy said. "I bet she feels terrible for taking advantage of us so badly."

Hearing his brother voice some of his dark thoughts made him feel even more embarrassed about the way he'd spoken to Susanna.

But before he could admit he'd been thinking much the same thing, their mother clapped her wooden spoon on the counter. From the time they were little boys, that had been their mother's favorite way to discipline them. She'd never struck them with that spoon, but that whack on the countertop had never failed to redirect their antics.

"Roy, you know a child isn't going to be responsible for her parents' financial decisions. No matter how upset you might be about the way things happened, it was no fault of hers."

"You're right, Mamm," Roy said automatically. "There's no need to start rapping counters with your spoon."

Their mother's lips twitched. "It still gets your attention."

"Sure it does."

That little exchange had hit Neil right in his chest. His mother was right. He and Roy hadn't had any say while their father was borrowing money and then putting the farm on the market. Why had he been so intent on making a young woman bear that burden?

What had he been thinking? Dale had been right. He should have turned around and apologized.

"You're looking a little peaked, brother," Roy said. "What happened?"

"I said some things I shouldn't have." Needing to unburden his heart, he said, "Mamm, I was pretty mean to her. She seemed so happy in our house, and she had no idea what the consequences were of her parents' actions."

"Isn't that how it always is, son?" Mamm said softly. "None of us ever really knows how what we do and what we say affects everyone around us. It's easy to make someone's day . . . or ruin it with just a few short words."

Now he felt even worse. He didn't think he had done anything that would have ruined Susanna's day, but he had started thinking that he probably wouldn't have been too upset if he had done that, either.

"One day we'll have our own place again," Roy said. "Then we'll be able to hold our heads up high."

"We already can. Don't you see?" Mamm asked. "It ain't

what we have or don't have that counts. What matters is how we follow our faith and treat others." Closing the tin, she smiled. "Especially at Christmastime, don't you think?"

Looking at each other, he and his brother shared a smile. "*Jah*, Mamm."

Right then and there, Neil's world opened to him again. His mother was exactly right. Dale had been, too. Once he put what was important in his life first, everything else fell into place. It was really rather miraculous.

"Next time I see her, I'll apologize," he promised.

"I hope so. I, for one, have had enough bad feelings and resentment. I'm ready to enjoy Christmas this year. Don't you think it's time we all started focusing on what is really important?"

"Of course, Mamm." Rolling up his sleeves, he said, "Now tell me how I can help you with all these cookies."

His mother's pleased chuckle was as welcome as the morning sun on his face.

CHAPTER 5

After much internal debate, Susanna elected not to share her troubling conversation with Neil with anyone besides Amanda. Their parents had enough to worry about without feeling guilty about something that wasn't their fault.

There wasn't anything they could do about it anyway. The sale had taken place. For better or worse, everyone had moved and was living in new homes. It wasn't like they could go back in time and handle the purchase of the Vances' house differently.

That was why on Monday, after helping their mother unpack the last of the cardboard boxes cluttering the back corner of the dining room, Susanna told her parents that she wanted to take advantage of the sunny day and run some errands with Amanda.

When a look of relief crossed her mother's face, Susanna had known she'd made the right decision. Ever since the accident, her mother had been worried about her health and her state of mind. Susanna knew why she felt that way. Back in Berlin, she'd been a busy woman, with lots of social engagements. Recovering at home with only her thoughts for company had been difficult for her.

Now that she had a better idea of what was behind everyone's standoffishness, Susanna knew that the only way to make things better was to move forward.

It turned out that their positive attitudes had propelled them toward a positive day. She and Amanda chatted with a few people they'd met at church outside of the entrance to the cave that gave the town its name. Horse Cave got the name because it was home to an actual underground cavern. It was a sizable place. Not as big as Mammoth Cave, of course, but the realtor had told them that the cave was under much of the heart of the town, with branches of it even snaking out for hundreds of yards in different directions. From the description they'd gotten, Susanna liked to imagine that the cave was shaped like a giant octopus underneath them.

But of course it wasn't called Octopus Cave. It was called Horse Cave because, folks said, outlaws used to hide their horses near the cave's entrance.

When they'd first arrived, their little sister, Traci, had wanted to visit it, but the rest of the family had overruled her suggestion. Going in a dark, damp cave in the winter didn't sound fun at all. Instead, they'd made plans to go in the summer when the cave would give them all a nice break from the hot temperatures outside.

The first thing Susanna and Amanda did on their trip into town was locate the library. After getting library cards, they bought necessities at the market, then stopped by a little café and ate hot cranberry scones and drank tea.

"This was a nice day, wasn't it?" Amanda asked when they had finished their errands and were on the way home.

Susanna nodded. "Getting out and doing something fun really brightened my spirits, especially since we are once again enjoying a break in the weather." It was true. After a quick burst of snow on Sunday evening, the sun had come out again. The day's sunny weather had even melted the snow on the blacktopped roads. It made getting around so much easier.

That said, taking only the main roads home was a long and meandering route. There was a shortcut through a section of the Kaufmann property that shortened the time home substantially. If they got to the path already made through the snowy field, they could make it to a picturesque bridge. That bridge, and the small creek that ran under it, was the dividing line between the two properties.

"You think it's okay if we walk on the Kaufmanns' property still?" Amanda asked as they approached the edge of the path.

"I think so. Dale seemed nice, like he wanted to get along with us."

Still Amanda hesitated. "Getting along and walking through their property seem like two different things. I'd hate for him to get mad at us. We need to make a good impression, not more of a bad one."

"It's heading toward four o'clock. We need to get home and help Mamm with supper," Susanna replied. "I think we should go ahead. Besides, it ain't like there are crops growing right now."

"That's true." But after they went about a hundred yards, Amanda tensed beside her. "Oh, no."

"What?" she asked, then noticed the two men walking toward them.

They had knit caps on their heads and thick black coats. Boots and scarves, too. They looked Amish from a distance, but it was impossible to know. And even if they were, it didn't mean that they were going to be real happy that they were walking in their field.

"Do you think that's Dale and his father or brother or something?"

"I don't know."

But as they got closer, a sinking feeling settled in her stomach. "That's Dale and Neil."

Amanda groaned. "This is going to be so awkward. We should have asked Dale for permission to walk here. I knew it."

Hearing Amanda's nervousness fueled Susanna's anger toward Neil Vance. Her sister was the most easygoing, perpetually happy person she'd ever met. For her to start fretting about whether or not she should walk somewhere said everything about how rudely they'd been treated since arriving in Horse Cave.

"This is ridiculous. We're supposed to start apologizing because we walked on a field covered in snow in the middle of winter? What could they be upset about?"

"They don't like us. They don't need a lot of reasons, Susanna."

Dale and Neil were now standing side by side, watching them approach. Dale looked friendly enough, while Neil's expression was blank. As they got closer, she realized that his knit cap was a dark navy and seemed to make his eyes look even bluer.

She wasn't sure what to think about noticing that!

"What should we say?" Amanda mumbled as they got closer.

"I don't know," she whispered back. Deciding to brazen it out, she waved a hand. "Hello!"

Dale raised a hand and smiled. "Hiya."

Neil didn't say a word. He just stood motionless and watched them approach. Suddenly, all her bluster seemed pretty childish. The fact of the matter was that she knew the Kaufmanns might not appreciate them walking through their private property, but she'd encouraged Amanda to do it anyway. Her mouth felt like a cup of cotton was in it. She honestly had no idea about what to say without making things worse.

Then, to her amazement, her sister strode forward, all smiles. "Hi. We didn't actually get to meet yesterday. I'm Amanda Schwartz."

And just like that, the tension evaporated. Dale smiled. "I'm Dale Kaufmann. This is Neil Vance."

"I was just telling Susanna how glad I am to see you. I hope you don't mind us cutting through your field. You don't mind, do you?" she asked before prattling on. "It makes the trek home so much easier and faster, especially in the winter."

Dale shrugged after a second's pause. "Not really. But seeing you ladies did catch me off guard."

Susanna decided it was time to take her medicine. "I'm afraid our being here is my fault. Our hands are filled and we were anxious to get home." Pointing to their footprints in the snow, she added, "Do you want us to turn around and walk back the way we came?"

Dale laughed. "Would you really do that?"

"Of course," Amanda said quickly. "We're your neighbors

now and we'll likely be seeing each other quite a bit. We want to get along, not be a thorn in your side."

Noticing a flicker of dismay in Neil's eyes, Susanna decided to take things a step further. "Or even more of a thorn than we already are, of course," she said.

Neil stepped forward. "About that. Listen, it was wrong of me to be so rude yesterday. I know my family's problems aren't your fault. I shouldn't have taken it out on you."

Susanna was so relieved, she almost teared up. She didn't know why, but she really didn't want Neil to think badly of her. "We've never had a farm before," she shared, wanting him to realize that her family weren't the spoiled, difficult people the girls at yesterday's lunch had made them out to be. "When we lived in Berlin, the five of us were in a duplex. But if we did have this farm, and then had to move off of it, I bet I would be upset, too."

Dale held out a hand. "Now that we've all apologized and feel better about things, how about we help you carry your bags home?"

"We couldn't let you do that," Amanda said, though her eyes were glowing.

"It's nothing. I'll even help you over this bridge. It gets icy from time to time in the winter."

After peeking over her shoulder at Susanna, Amanda handed Dale two of her bags and started walking next to his side.

"You don't have to walk me or carry my bags," Susanna said. "I'll be fine."

"I don't mind helping you, either," Neil said as he reached out to grasp the handles of her two bags. As he did so, his bare fingertips brushed against hers. She felt a little burst of awareness that confused her.

She firmly tamped that down. As they started walking, she said, "I feel like I should keep apologizing to you. Or make amends or something. You rescued me, but I'm living in your farmhouse."

"In our old house. And I agree with Dale. Let's drop the subject."

"All right," Susanna said as she became aware that while she and Neil were having a difficult and somewhat awkward conversation, that was not the case with her sister and Dale.

They were walking along as if they were old friends.

"THEY SEEM TO be off on the right foot," Neil said to Susanna as they walked behind Dale and her sister.

Watching Amanda smile up at Dale, and even say something that made him laugh, Susanna swallowed awkwardly. "They do. Um, Amanda has that way about her, though. She is so bright and cheerful. Most everyone enjoys her company."

"What about you?"

"Me?"

"*Jah*. Does everyone enjoy your company, too?"

What did he mean by that? She darted a quick glance at him, hoping to ascertain whether he was simply making conversation or whether he was being sarcastic. "I'm not sure what you mean," she said at last.

"I guess I deserved that. You don't know whether to trust me or not."

That was true. She didn't. He was so serious, and he'd been so angry about her family living in his old house. But it was time to move on. If he could reach out to make amends, so could she. "I want to trust you," she finally said.

"How do ya think we can make it happen?"

She glanced at him again. His expression was earnest. "Maybe we simply resolve to start thinking the best of each other."

"I'd like that," he said.

"Me, too," she said sincerely. She would love to have the tension that she'd been feeling between their two families lessen.

"Do you think we're going to be okay now?" he asked after they'd gone a couple of feet. "If I see you on the street, you won't ignore me, will you?"

"Of course not." Seeking to tease him a bit, she said, "Just you wait, I'll march right up to you and say hello."

He laughed. "You know what? I can actually picture you doing that. I'll look forward to it."

This was the first time she'd heard him laugh. It sounded good, almost infectious. She almost told him so, but knew stating such a thing would be too much. Too forward. Instead, she pointed to the arched wooden bridge in front of them. "That's a lovely little bridge. Did you build it?" It arched over a small winding creek. She imagined the creek wouldn't be too hard to cross in the middle of summer when the water level was sure to be low. But now it was filled with a good bit of snow and ice.

"Me and Dale patched it up a couple of years ago, but my grandfather was the one who originally built it. Don't worry, though. It's a little creaky but in good repair."

"I'm sure it's fine," she said with a smile as she stepped on the first plank. But then, of course, all her hope for looking poised went out the window when her boot slipped on the slick surface.

"Here, let me help you." He reached for her elbow with his free hand.

"*Danke*," she whispered.

"It's no trouble. I'd hate for you to fall off the bridge."

"Me, too."

When they reached the end of the bridge, she was sure that he would release her arm and step away. But he kept close by her side, her arm firmly in his clasp.

"We're off the bridge now, you know."

"*Jah*. But these fields can be slick sometimes, too. Especially when the snow starts to melt in the middle of winter. Little air pockets form underneath the surface of the top layer of ice. I'm thinking it would be a good idea if we stayed close to each other until we get back on the path. I've had more than one misstep over the years."

Susanna doubted that. Neil was so assured, so confident, she couldn't imagine his body betraying him like that. No doubt he played, ran, and walked across them more times than he could count. So the right thing to do would be to pull away from his side and assure him that she didn't need his help.

But for some reason, she wasn't in any hurry to do that. Maybe it was because he was taking care to keep his voice soft and easy, like he didn't want to spook her.

Or maybe it was because he was speaking to her like she was worth his patience and care. It was such a nice change. Looking up into his face, she tried to think of something to say.

"Sue, you ready to go?" Amanda asked.

"What? Oh! *Jah*. Sure." Quickly, she pulled her arm out of Neil's grasp. He released it immediately. "We need to head in and help with supper," she said.

"Of course."

Susanna took a couple of steps, then gave in to temptation and glanced back at Neil. He was standing next to Dale. Both of them were watching. Then, almost imperceptibly, Dale nodded at her.

Feeling like something important had just happened, she nodded in return, and then followed Amanda back to the house.

Only when they were walking toward the back door to the substantial mudroom, where they could remove their wet boots and clothes, did Amanda speak.

"This has been quite a day, don't you think?"

"*Jah*. An eventful one, for sure."

"Do you think we should tell Mamm and Daed about walking with Neil and Dale?"

"Maybe only that they seemed nice," she said at last. "No need for them to ever know how Neil and I got off to a rough start."

After a moment's pause, Amanda nodded. "I think you have a good point. They've got enough to worry about."

Susanna smiled. "This is true. Besides, with Christmas just around the corner, it's only right that we start over fresh."

CHAPTER 6

Thursday, December 14

Several days after she and Neil had resolved to start over, Susanna put most of her worries about him behind her. It felt good to wake up in the morning with a clear head and heart.

It also felt good to settle back into her regular routine of helping her mother as much as possible. While Mamm seemed to be feeling strong, all of them still worried about her. Susanna knew that she would never forget sitting by her mother's side in the hospital and listening to the doctor explain that her mother's pneumonia had been aggravated by stress and exhaustion.

Ever since that scary afternoon, she'd vowed to take on more of the household responsibilities.

They'd spent the majority of the afternoon working in the kitchen, both preparing a few dishes to freeze and making the evening's meal of stuffed peppers.

But while Susanna had been content to slice and dice in the quiet, her mother had seemed preoccupied. When they were almost done, she cleared her throat. "Susanna, what is going on with your sister? Do you know?"

Susanna made a show of shoving her wooden spoon around the browning hamburger and onions in the pan. "Which one?"

"Amanda, of course. We both know Traci is fine."

"Amanda? Hmm. I don't know."

Her mother clicked her tongue as she turned back to the tomato sauce she was stirring. But it was obvious that she didn't believe Susanna for a second. "She's been going out walking by herself. Do you know anything about that?"

She did. Amanda had shared that she had met Dale on those walks. But that wasn't Susanna's news to share.

"When I peeked in the living room, she wasn't sewing. She was simply staring out the window."

"Maybe she was looking at cardinals?" Ack. Could she have not thought of a better excuse?

"*Nee*, child. She was not bird-watching."

Turning off the gas burner, Susanna set the frying pan to one side. "I'm sure Amanda is fine, Mamm. Please don't worry."

As she always did, her mother thought about that answer. Then she shook her head. "Something is bothering her and I know you know what it is. You might as well tell me. Is she still unhappy about the move?"

"I think she's settling in." Actually, Susanna was pretty sure Amanda was settling in a little bit too much. Ever since Dale had walked her home from the bridge, Amanda had acted distracted. She was smitten.

"When I asked her what she was looking at, Amanda just blinked at me, like she didn't know how to respond."

Susanna was beginning to not know how to answer her mother, either. To give herself more time, she combined the sauce and meat mixture, then began to stuff the peppers she'd hollowed out earlier that day.

"Susanna, I think she was searching for something in particular." She wrinkled her nose. "But what could it be? There's not much to see except snow."

"Maybe she saw a deer? Or, um, a rabbit? You know how pretty they look against the snow-covered fields."

"She was never all that excited about woodland creatures, Sue." Her mother's tone had more than a good bit of sarcasm in it. Yet another reminder that she never had been the type of woman who was easy to fool.

Just as she had never been the type of woman who was good at dodging questions or telling fibs. Tired of making the attempt, Susanna said, "Why don't you ask her?"

"I did. But she—" Mamm stopped abruptly when the back door to the mudroom opened with a slam. Together, Susanna and her mother turned in surprise.

When Daed entered the kitchen, tracking wet dirt and snow behind him, her mother groaned. "Do you see the mess you're making on my floors? Honestly, John. I just—"

"We've got a problem, Leah," he interrupted. "Part of the back fence was broken last night. Someone demolished a good six-foot section of the fencing. It's in pieces all over the ground."

"My word!" Mamm exclaimed. Walking to his side, she said, "What do you think could have done that? Was it a bear or something?"

"It weren't no bear."

Still wondering why her father was so upset, Susanna said,

"We had some strong winds last night. Maybe that shook some of the boards loose."

"Maybe so," Mamm said. "You know what? Sue and I were just standing here, talking about deer. Maybe a buck could have broken it. You know how much damage those deer can do."

Daed shook his head. "That damage wasn't caused by the wind, and it certainly wasn't caused by some deer. And it wasn't an accident, either. I think someone went on our property, took out a sledgehammer, and deliberately broke a good six feet of the fencing."

Susanna knew her father wasn't the type of man to exaggerate, but that did seem a little bit farfetched. Still attempting to be helpful, she offered, "Well, you know how teens are. Maybe a couple of kids were out walking and got rowdy." Of course, the moment she said that, she felt foolish. Rowdy teens did not wander around farms with sledgehammers breaking fences. No one was that bored.

"This wasn't caused by teens running around, Sue." Sitting down, he sighed. "As much as it pains me to say this, I think someone broke our fencing on purpose."

Her mother was looking increasingly flustered. "But why? We just moved here. We haven't done anything to anyone."

Her father sighed. "You know how cool everyone has acted toward us. I didn't want to upset you girls, but I think a lot of people are mad that we bought this property."

"It was for sale," Mamm pointed out. "They should be happy because we bought it."

"I know that. But sometimes people twist things in their heads," Daed said.

"Say someone *was* upset. Breaking fencing doesn't seem like a smart way to deal with that anger."

Susanna cleared her throat. "Um, Mamm, Daed, I'm afraid there might be something to this. Several women told Amanda and me that lots of people think we took advantage of the Vances by buying the farm at such a low price. Then, well, I talked to Neil Vance at church. He kind of confirmed that his family has been upset about how the sale was handled."

Daed glared. "You heard all that at church?"

"*Jah.*"

"And all this time you didn't feel the need to share that information with your mother and myself?"

"I didn't want to upset you or Mamm. Besides, Amanda and I saw Neil and Dale Kaufmann on Monday when we were walking home. We talked for a while, and patched things up."

Mamm groaned. "And you didn't think to mention that either?"

"I'm sorry?"

"Is that why Amanda keeps looking out the window? Is she afraid of those boys?"

Oh, this was a mess! "*Nee . . .*"

Her mother folded her arms over her chest. "Susanna, I've had enough of your talking in circles. Please, just give us some information without making us play twenty questions."

Mentally apologizing to her sister, she said, "Amanda isn't looking out the window because she's afraid. She's looking out the window because Dale hinted that he might stop by. She likes him."

"*That* is what is wrong?" Mamm groaned.

"I told you she was fine, Mother."

"Oh, for heaven's sakes. You girls never fail to surprise me," Daed said with a groan. Susanna knew he wasn't too upset because there was a new bit of light in his eyes. "You know what? I think it's time we went over to our neighbors and introduced ourselves. Maybe I'm blowing things out of proportion and there's an obvious reason for that broken fence. Maybe they know what happened to it."

"Amanda did say that Dale's parents wished they'd already come here to welcome us," Susanna said.

"The decision is made, then." Turning to Susanna, Mamm said, "You'd best go fetch your sisters and share our plans for the evening."

"We're all going to go?" asked Susanna.

Her mother nodded. "I think so. It's time we reached out to folks, even if they haven't been reaching out to us. I'll even bring a pecan pie."

Daed's eyes twinkled. "And while we're there, we can meet Dale."

"Don't tell Amanda I told you about him. She's going to be so mad if she finds out."

Her mother laughed. "She'll be fine. All you have to do is tell her that I wore you down. She'll believe that."

Susanna chuckled, too. Amanda would believe that without question. Their mother was extremely skilled at wheedling information from them. "After I talk to Amanda and Traci, I'll come back to help you with the pie."

"*Danke*, Sue."

Leaving her parents to discuss what they were going to say, Susanna informed Traci, who was in the basement working on laundry, then walked to the back room, where Amanda was sewing.

The moment she saw Susanna, she hastily hid her project.

"What are you working on?" Susanna asked.

"Something for Christmas. What do you need?"

"Only to tell you that we'll be going over to the Kaufmanns' *haus* tonight." While Amanda gaped at her, Susanna filled her in on their father's news about the broken fence line and the plan to visit the Kaufmanns' house after supper.

As she anticipated, her sister's expression shone with different emotions. "Do you need help with the pie?"

"Absolutely not."

Amanda laughed. "That's what I hoped you'd say. I'll finish this project, then go see how I can help Mamm or Daed. Then, I think I might go ahead and wash my hair."

"You're going to wash it this afternoon?"

"Of course. I won't want to wash it when we get home. It might be late."

Yep, Amanda was definitely infatuated with their new charming neighbor. Smitten enough that she probably wouldn't even care if the whole household knew who occupied her thoughts. That was a relief, indeed.

CHAPTER 7

Thursday, December 14

It had been a long day. Neil had volunteered to come in early to work to help Junior, his boss at Horse Cave Salvage, re-organize the bulk-food aisle. Flour, sugar, and popcorn fairly flew off the shelves this time of the year.

After he carefully followed Junior's directives, he'd gone out in a truck to help with deliveries. Of course, they'd gotten stuck in traffic and had returned almost an hour late.

All that meant he was walking home right as the sun was setting. It was going to be a race to see if he could walk in his door before it was pitch-black outside.

Just as he approached the entrance to his uncle's land, he spied Uncle Joseph himself on the front porch. He was sitting in one of the five Adirondack chairs decorating the area. His feet were resting on the porch railing and he was smoking a cigarette. A large metal kerosene lamp rested on the table nearby.

Though Neil would have preferred to walk on by, common

courtesy—and his family's gratitude—dictated that he approach and at least say hello.

"*Gut ohvet*, Onkle," he called out.

"Good evening to you, too," Joseph said as he got to his feet. "You are getting home late. Ain't so?"

"I am. I'm grateful for the work, though."

"*Jah*. Work is always a blessing." Joseph leaned against one of the square columns decorating his expansive front porch. His relaxed posture was a marked contrast to his words.

Actually, many things about Joseph were contradictory.

Looking at him in the dim light, Neil figured if he didn't know better, one would think his uncle was English. His hair was cut short, he had no beard, since he was unmarried, and his clothes, though technically plain, were definitely sewn from expensive fabric. His fondness for smoking was also rare in the Amish community. It wasn't forbidden—many men smoked pipes—but his fondness for his red pack of cigarettes was notable.

"Would you like to join me for a bit?" Joseph asked. "I made some fresh *kaffi*."

He didn't want to. But here his uncle had given them so much. How could he refuse? "*Danke.*"

Looking pleased, Joseph extinguished his cigarette. "Have a seat. I'll be right back. You take it black, yes?"

"*Jah*," he said as his uncle strode into the house. Before sitting down, Neil glanced around the side of the house. In the distance, about a mile up the drive, stood the house he was now living in. Multiple lights shone through the windows. Smoke rose from the chimney. It looked like everyone was home, either eating or visiting together around the fireplace. He longed to join them.

But surely it was good he was spending some time with his uncle, too? How many evenings had Joseph spent in this same spot, watching all of them together while he smoked his cigarettes alone?

"Here you go," Joseph said as he strode back outside with two large white ceramic mugs in his hands. As he passed Neil his, he said, "Some people complain that coffee keeps them up at night, but it never affects me."

"Me, neither," Neil said, though he couldn't actually remember the last time he'd sipped coffee so late in the day.

Joseph sat down, shook out another cigarette, and lit it with a sigh. "I'm glad you stopped to say hello, Neil. Most times you don't."

What could he say to that? "Usually, I'm anxious to take a shower and eat . . ."

"And there is only one shower in that house. No doubt hot water is at a premium." He grinned at his joke.

Neil grinned uncomfortably. There was a note in his uncle's tone that sounded like he was talking about something other than just hot water.

As he tapped his cigarette on the edge of the ashtray, Joseph murmured, "I bet you are missing your house. There was a lot of space there. I mean, from what I remember. Three bathrooms on the second floor alone."

Feeling more ill at ease, Neil sipped his coffee. "We are fine where we are."

"No, you're not." After placing his cup on the table, he turned to face Neil more directly. "You don't even have a bedroom now, do you?"

"I do not."

"Where do you sleep?"

Neil knew Joseph was aware of their sleeping arrangements. He had brought it up on purpose, just to stir the pot. But even though Neil knew that, he still answered. Joseph had done a lot for their family and deserved his respect. "Me and Roy are sleeping on the floor in the living room."

Looking even more pensive, Joseph blew out a plume of smoke. "Here you are, a grown man, a man working ten, eleven hours a day . . . reduced to sleeping on the floor of his living room. Such a waste."

"I am fine, Onkle."

"I suppose your *bruder* is, too?"

Neil nodded. After all, what could he say? It was because of their uncle's generosity that they had a place to live at all.

But his lack of complaint only seemed to make his uncle even more frustrated. "Did you know that I offered to have you and Roy move in with me?"

Neil was shocked. So shocked, he shook his head.

"I didn't think so. Your father refused to consider the idea, even though I have plenty of room. Even though I would have appreciated the company. Even though I've done so much for you all over the years . . ." His chair creaked as he stamped out his smoke. "But it was never enough, I guess. I wonder why."

"You don't understand why?" His voice was strained. Hoarse.

"What reason could your father have for refusing my invitation? Was it simply pride . . . or did he think your living arrangements were only temporary?"

Yet again, it seemed as if Uncle Joseph was speaking of more than one thing. But instead of helping him understand his father's point of view, it only made Neil feel more uncomfortable. And vaguely disloyal.

Needing to put some space between them, Neil surged to his feet. "*Danke* for the *kaffi*. But I need to go home now."

Uncle Joseph laughed. "Sorry. I guess I'm telling you things I shouldn't."

"It's not that. It's that my father should be here for this discussion, too."

"I guess you would feel that way. I don't blame you. It's hard to know who to trust anymore, isn't it?"

"Good night, Uncle."

"*Jah.* Have a good night, Neil. Sleep well." His uncle's words rang in his head as Neil started down the black asphalt driveway. Had Joseph been trying to say that he didn't trust his father? And if that was the case . . . why did it not feel all that shocking?

AS THE FOUR of them walked neatly in a line behind their father and his flashlight, each of the women taking care to step in his large footprints in the ankle-deep snow, Susanna thought they probably looked like a line of ducks.

That, or maybe a little train, she mused whimsically, given the fact that they had walked like this many a time. Over the years, the five of them had delivered pies or crocheted blankets or other small gifts to neighbors many times. It was nice to do something for other people, but they actually enjoyed doing things together. They were a close-knit family and always had been. Even though their *daed* had worked away from home, they'd still managed to be closer than most.

It was one of the reasons Susanna had accompanied her whole family south to Kentucky without a second's thought. No matter what opportunities might have arisen in Berlin, she felt the same way that her parents did, that after their faith, family came first.

She supposed Neil felt that way about his family, too. Of course, he would side with them if his parents thought her parents had mishandled the purchase of their property. But as she thought of their conversation on their way home the other day, Susanna felt that things were changing for the better. She, at least, was learning more about Neil as a person— and she liked the things she was discovering about him. She liked that he worked hard and was so serious. She was that way, too.

"We're almost there," Amanda whispered, interrupting her thoughts.

"That we are."

"Do you think Dale is going to be home?" she asked. Her eyes were wide with anticipation.

She looked so cute, so, well, smitten, that Susanna was finding it hard to keep a straight face. "I guess we're going to find out soon."

"I hope he is," she said with a smile.

As she watched her sister from behind, Susanna grinned at the way Amanda seemed to have a new bounce to her step. She couldn't help but feel a little jealous. Amanda's feelings for the neighbor were honest and wide open. Out there for anyone to see. From the looks of things, it had seemed that Dale felt the same way.

It seemed Dale had no qualms about separating his sadness about the Vances leaving from his admiration for Amanda.

She hoped he would continue to act the same way in front of his family, even after their father shared the disturbing news about the broken fence.

What if he acted noticeably cooler? Amanda would be so embarrassed and hurt. She shivered, thinking how painful that would be to watch.

"Are you shivering, Sue?" Traci asked.

"What? Oh, maybe a little. I should have worn another scarf," Susanna said. "How cold is it, do you think?"

"Only in the twenties," Amanda said over her shoulder.

"Cold enough."

Traci trotted up to her side. "*Jah*, but it ain't all that cold. You're so silly, Sue. You always complain about the winter weather."

It was kind of true. While everyone else seemed to take the winter weather in stride, Susanna always was whining about how wet and cold she was. Eyeing the well-kept farmhouse they were approaching, she said, "Look, we're almost there. They have a pretty home, don't they?"

"It is. I like their green metal roof. Look! They have a gazebo. I bet that's pretty in the summer."

Amanda smiled. "I bet it is."

Susanna noticed that her response was slightly hesitant. "Are you worried about this visit?"

"A little bit."

"Me, too," Susanna agreed. "The last thing we need is another family being upset with us."

"Hopefully that won't be the case," Amanda said.

"Well, I hope the Kaufmanns let us stay for a bit and warm up," Susanna quipped, attempting to lighten their worries.

Amanda giggled. "Me, too."

"Stop complaining, girls," Daed called out.

"I'm not complaining," Traci said. "Amanda and Susanna are arguing. Not me."

"We weren't arguing," Amanda said.

"All of you, hush," Mamm chided. "Instead of snipping and snapping at each other, you should be hoping we have a good and productive visit."

"I don't think there's anything wrong with hoping it's a good, productive, and *warm* one," said Susanna.

"Oh, brother," Mamm said. "Some things never change, do they? Once again, you are making sure you get your last word in."

"I'm not quite that bad," Susanna protested.

"There she goes again," muttered Traci.

"I, for one, am rather enjoying this little walk. It feels familiar and so many other things haven't lately," Amanda commented. "After all, we've certainly delivered a gift together a time or two."

"Or maybe twenty-two," Susanna said.

"It's been more than that," Traci said.

As they walked up the short brick-lined walkway, Daed shook his head. "Sometimes you girls sound exactly as you did when you were twelve. It never ceases to amaze me. Now, put on your good manners."

"Sorry, Daed," Amanda said. "I'll do my best."

"I bet you will," Susanna whispered.

Amanda blushed. But before she could say anything, the front door opened.

And then there stood Dale Kaufmann. "Hello," he said. He stared curiously at her parents, smiled hesitantly at Traci and Susanna, then settled on Amanda. "Hi."

Amanda smiled brightly. As if he'd just said something amazing and insightful. "Hiya, Dale. We, um, we came over to say hello. We brought you a pie, too."

"That's kind of you. Ain't so?" he asked as he turned around.

Susanna had been so intent on watching the interplay of her sister and Dale, the crowd of people standing behind him took her by surprise.

After the briefest of pauses, a lovely woman with Dale's brown eyes and hair approached. "*Wilcom*. I'm Anna Kaufmann," she said as she opened the door wider. "It's so kind of you to come over. Please, do come in."

"*Danke*," Daed said, walking through and stopping politely so he didn't track snow on the clean floors.

Just as Susanna was taking off her cloak, she noticed Amanda and Dale were staring at each other. Just like the rest of them didn't exist.

It was so personal, so intimate, she felt her cheeks heat.

It seemed she hadn't needed to be worried about Dale Kaufmann ignoring her sister after all. Instead, she should have been worried about the sparks that were flying between the two of them.

CHAPTER 8

Thursday Evening, December 14

As his parents led the way to their family room and two of his sisters hastily ran into the kitchen to brew coffee and pull out plates and forks for the pie, Dale Kaufmann tried to get his mind centered.

He needed to act calm and thoughtful, but he feared that was doomed to be an insurmountable task. After all, he was as much at a loss for how to deal with their unexpected visitors as anyone else in his ten-person family. His parents, never ones for surprises, were visibly dismayed.

And his younger siblings? Well, they could hardly contain themselves. They were whispering to each other, some excitedly, some with far less enthusiastic expressions.

Mr. Schwartz seemed thoughtful and intent. His wife acted nervous. Susanna seemed quiet. The littlest one seemed that way, too.

Then he focused on Amanda. She raised her blue eyes to him. Smiled just slightly.

Suddenly, he was tongue-tied.

As if she realized this, her smile grew.

He needed to say something, anything, so everyone wouldn't notice that he was simply standing there staring at her. Like a besotted fool. "Hiya, Amanda. How have you been?"

A glimmer in her eyes let him know that his comment sounded as inane as he'd feared. "I am fine. And you?"

Considering that he had spent far too many hours thinking about her and was now fumbling for conversation, he shrugged. "All right."

"Ah."

"Amanda?" Susanna called out. "Let's sit down."

She edged away from him. "I better sit down."

"*Jah*. Me, too." *Good gravy!* Was he incapable of saying anything worthwhile?

After offering their visitors a seat, Dale's father folded his hands in his lap. "John, Leah, it was good of you to come over. We thank you for the pie, too."

"We should have come over before now."

"*Nee*," Dale's mother said. "We should have been more welcoming." After sharing a look with his father, Mamm said, "The fault lies with me, I suppose. I grew up in this house, and lived next to the Vances all my life. It was hard to see them go. I'm afraid I've been mourning the loss."

"We've noticed that a lot of people have had a hard time with us moving here," Mr. Schwartz said.

"I canna deny that," Daed said simply. Dale was glad that his father hadn't tried to soften his words or make up some explanation. It was better to be open and honest instead of tacking on cumbersome explanations that were not completely true.

Unable to help himself, he glanced toward Amanda. She was sitting quietly next to her sister, her blond, blue-eyed, wholesome looks complementing her sister's darker hair and green eyes. Both women were so pretty. Their little sister was sitting near Jimmy, Michael, and Avery, Dale's youngest siblings. The four of them were quietly whispering to each other, no doubt wishing they were doing something else.

Luckily, Beth and Esther brought in a tray loaded with coffee cups, pie plates, some fingerprint cookies the girls had made that afternoon, and silverware. Marie, all of fifteen, looked pleased to be carrying the coffeepot instead of having to sit with her younger siblings. The next ten minutes were spent passing out cups of coffee, doing the same with the pie, then complimenting the snacks.

As Dale took a big bite of pie, smiling at his sisters when Mrs. Schwartz shared that Susanna had made it, he couldn't help but reflect that he and his family had sat in the room with his neighbors many, many times over the years.

Of course, it had been a different family, and they'd all been so comfortable with each other that it hadn't felt as if they'd had company over at all.

He and Neil had often sat in the background, sneaking cookies that their mothers pretended they didn't see them eat, whispering and joking to each other, making plans for Christmas break, for summer breaks. Making plans for the rest of their lives.

Dale realized then that he might be twenty-five years old, but it was the first time that he'd come to terms with the fact that his future was going to be different than the one he and Neil had planned. They weren't going to be farming next to each other. They weren't going to be living next to each other for the rest of their lives. Their future had changed.

Now, as he sipped his coffee, he realized that though their future was going to be different, he wasn't mourning the loss anymore. Instead, he had accepted it.

He was grateful for that. He—and his whole family—needed to move forward. God gave them a lifetime to live for a reason. He didn't intend for every day to be the same as the one before.

Mr. Schwartz cleared his throat. After looking at his wife, he set his coffee cup down and pressed his palms on his knees.

"Anna and Jeremy, thank you for your hospitality. Being here on this snowy evening does my heart good. I know I speak for all five of us when I say that it has meant a lot to us."

Mamm's cheeks flushed. "It was our pleasure. Like we said, we should have paid you a visit when you first moved in."

"I must admit that we came over for another reason."

The whole room tensed. Even Dale's thirteen-year-old brother, Jimmy, who rarely listened to anyone besides himself.

"What is it?" Daed asked.

"When I was out today, along the south end of my property, where it connects with yours . . ."

"Yes?"

"I discovered that part of the fencing was broken."

Relieved that fencing was all that was on his mind, Dale exhaled. "That happens from time to time. It's old wood, you know. Sometimes the winter storms wreak havoc and cause the fencing to splinter like toothpicks. I'll help you fix it in the morning."

"*Danke*, son," his father said. "I know you'll do a good job of repairs."

But instead of looking grateful, Mr. Schwartz only seemed more agitated. "You all are misunderstanding me. Forgive me if I sound harsh, but I ain't talking about a piece of broken wood. I managed a large farm for most of my life. I know how to mend fencing, and I'm familiar with the usual wear and tear that occurs over years."

"Then I'm afraid I don't understand," his *daed* said.

"I'm saying I discovered a six-foot section that is in splinters."

"Splinters?" Max, Dale's older brother, asked.

Mr. Schwartz nodded. "I'm afraid it's so badly damaged that it had to have been done on purpose."

Daed's eyebrows knit together. "Hopefully that ain't the case. Sometimes animals get spooked and break through fencing, you know."

"When you see it, I think you'll agree that no animal is to blame."

Unable to help himself, Dale stood up. "But it all doesn't make sense. Why would anyone want to ruin good fencing?"

"That's what I wanted to ask you. Do you have any idea about why someone would deliberately damage my property?"

"The fence is technically on both of our properties," Max said.

Mr. Schwartz looked from Max to their father to Dale. "Well, I sure didn't break it, and I know my girls didn't, either."

Mamm flushed. "Are you accusing us?"

"I am not," Mr. Schwartz said slowly, though his expression told a different story. "However, I must admit that this whole situation does cause me concern. If you say that nothing like this has ever occurred, then it does after we move in a few weeks ago . . ."

"No one in my family is going to go around breaking fences," Mr. Kaufmann said angrily. "I don't know how your neighbors back in Berlin treated you, but here in Kentucky, we got better things to do than destroy each other's property."

"I brought my family over here in order to discuss this with you, not point fingers. We don't want any trouble, either."

"Are you sure about that?"

Dale knew it was time to intervene. His father had a temper on his best day. He also had a habit of saying things that he later regretted. This was looking to be one of those moments.

"Mamm," he muttered. "Get Daed to calm down."

She met his eyes and nodded. "Everyone, I think it's time we all step back and take a deep breath. Don't you agree, Leah?"

Mrs. Schwartz's gaze warmed. "I agree one hundred percent. Nothing will get better if we remain angry. It would be far better for us to reach a place where we can all get along." Smiling softly, she added, "We want to be your neighbors for years and years. I'd like to get off on the right foot."

"Exactly," Mamm said.

To Dale's relief, his father exhaled, then looked a little sheepish. "I'm sorry. My temper's been a real fault of mine for all my life. I like to think that I've gotten a handle on it and learned to think before speaking . . . but obviously, that ain't the case."

"I could have probably broached the subject better, too," Mr. Schwartz said. "I shouldn't have come over without notice."

Mamm gestured to Marie. "Would anyone like more *kaffi*?"

When Mr. and Mrs. Schwartz both accepted, Dale knew

it was time to take a break. Turning toward Amanda, he said, "Would you like to go out to the back porch? It's a little chilly but there's a gas heater there." It went without saying that there was a lot more privacy, too.

"I'd like that," Amanda said. After a pause, she said, "Susanna, do you want to come, too?"

"*Nee*. I'll stay here and visit with the other girls."

As Dale helped Amanda dig out her cloak and put it on, he caught sight of both sets of parents watching his actions with interest.

Feeling like they were on display, he felt his cheeks flush. But that didn't stop him from pulling on his own coat and escorting her out the door. He was eager to spend more time with Amanda. And even though there was a faint shadow over this visit, he wasn't going to let the opportunity to be alone with her slip by.

He'd take time with Amanda Schwartz any way he could.

CHAPTER 9

Thursday Evening, December 14

Would it be wrong of me to say that I'm almost glad that fence broke?" Dale asked as he closed the door behind them.

Amanda couldn't help herself. She giggled like a teenager. "*Jah*. It would be wrong. That fencing is a serious matter." But yet, here she was, smiling, too.

He chuckled. "Of course, you are right."

She was so glad he'd brought out a lantern with them. It made her feel more at ease around him. It also gave her a good opportunity to study his features a little better. He really was so handsome. "Your sisters seem nice. All of your family does."

"We get along. Well, most of the time. There's a lot of us, you know."

"Eight *kinner* is an awful lot."

"Soon only seven of us will be living at home. My older brother, Max, is moving to Michigan."

"Why there?"

"His girlfriend's family just moved there. They're getting married soon."

"That's wonderful!" she exclaimed, just as she realized that sounding so happy about a sibling moving away was in bad taste. "Or, um, are you sad that he's going to move so far away?"

"*Nee*, I'm happy for him. We've always gotten along, but I've never been as close to him as I am to some of my sisters. Or Neil. Neil and I grew up together like brothers."

Amanda knew that he'd brought Neil Vance up in an innocent way. But still the mention of his name stung. "Well, um, congratulations anyway."

Stepping closer, he shook his head. "I didn't mention Neil in order to make you uncomfortable. I mentioned him because he's simply a part of my life. I know he got off on the wrong foot with your sister, but I promise, he's really not bad. He's actually a really good person. He's been a great friend to me over the years."

"I'm sure he has been." Because he was still staring at her intently, she said, "I'm sorry, I don't know how to make things easier between us."

"Maybe it already is. Maybe I'm hoping you'll see that I've come to terms with him moving."

She wished the lantern's glow was a little brighter. She would have loved to study his expression better. "Truly?"

"I promise. Now, if I tell you something else, will you listen to it with an open mind?"

She wondered what he could possibly say. "I'll try."

"Well, I've started to be very thankful that you moved here. Now I can start visiting you in the evenings."

Visiting in the evenings? "That sounds like you intend to be courting."

"That's probably because I'd like to. Eventually. When we know each other better. If you are okay with that."

Though he was stumbling over his words, she noticed that he also sounded hopeful. And, perhaps, a bit too sure of himself?

She couldn't resist teasing him a bit. "I might be . . . if my parents are okay as well." Primly, she added, "I'm sure you will be wanting their approval, too."

"Oh! *Jah*," he blurted, sounding slightly flustered. "To be sure. I am hoping that your parents will be open to my visits."

Now she was the one stepping closer to him. "I was only teasing you, Dale. If they hadn't been open to you calling on me, they would have never simply stood still and watched us step out here together."

"Did you notice that mine did the same?"

"I did." She smiled. "I know we don't really know each other all that well, but perhaps the two of us might help pave the way for our two families to learn to trust each other and get along."

"I hope so. If someone has decided to start breaking our fencing, we all are going to have to stand together. Otherwise, things will only get worse."

LATER THAT NIGHT, when Amanda was still lying on her back and staring at the ceiling, Susanna creaked open her door.

"Manda, you asleep?" she whispered.

"Nope."

"*Gut.*" After closing the door behind her, Susanna padded across the room and then hopped onto the other side of Amanda's big double bed. "I couldn't sleep, either."

Amanda moved onto her side to face her sister. "This is one of those times that I wish we still shared a room."

Chuckling softly, Susanna whispered, "I know. Who would have thought we would miss our little cramped room?"

Oh, but their room had been stuffed to the gills. Susanna was a pack rat, and she? Well, she always had boxes and bins of fabric or yarn that she was working on. When they were teenagers, they would argue about each other's stuff all the time.

But they'd also had each other all the time. They'd always talked about everything, late into the night. Their friends, their parents, how annoying Traci had been when she was seven . . .

Learning to go to sleep with only her thoughts had been difficult to get used to.

"What did you think about tonight?" Susanna asked.

"I don't know. The Kaufmanns seemed nice."

"Do you think Mamm and Daed are ever going to get along with them?"

"I hope so," mused Amanda. *Especially since Dale has such grand plans.*

"Mamm seemed happy when we got home."

"I thought so, too. Daed is still worried, but I'm glad he and Mr. Kaufmann are going to look at the damages together tomorrow."

"Jah." Susanna yawned. "So . . . how was Dale?"

She couldn't resist smiling. "He was good."

"Do you like him?"

"We just met!"

"I know. But do you like him?"

Looking into her sister's eyes, Amanda saw interest and humor. And love and acceptance. "*Jah*," she whispered.

Susanna smiled as she shifted to her back and closed her eyes. "His sister Esther told me that Dale really likes you. Isn't that something?"

A little shiver ran through her. "*Jah*," she whispered after a bit. "It's really something, indeed." After trying to stifle a yawn, she said, "'Night, Sue."

But her sister was already asleep.

Rolling over, Amanda closed her eyes and, finally sure she was going to have sweet dreams, let slumber find her, too.

CHAPTER 10

Sunday, December 17

The next few days passed uneventfully, and Susanna was thankful for that. Their father had gone out with Mr. Kaufmann, Dale, and his brother Max to the fencing the morning after their visit.

As soon as they'd seen the damage, the other men had wholeheartedly agreed with her father that someone had inflicted that damage on purpose. After some discussion, they'd elected not to go to the authorities about it. There wasn't anything anyone could do without evidence. The men rebuilt the fence, determined to view the damage as simply a random act of violence.

Now it was Sunday, and they were at another family's house for church. But this time, instead of sitting by themselves, Susanna and her sisters had sat with the Kaufmann girls. Afterward, the luncheon had gone well, too. Charity and the other women who had been so wary with them a week ago had greeted them pleasantly and had even invited Susanna and Amanda to join them again. After a few minutes of awkward conversation, they'd settled into an animated discussion about Christmas plans, gifts they were each making, and one couple's recent engagement.

Before long, Susanna and Amanda had been sharing as much as the other women. By the time they'd helped clean up the tables and washed some of the dishes that would go back in the church wagon, they'd even made some tentative plans to attend a gathering at a newly married couple's home one day before Christmas.

By the time two o'clock arrived, most people were either walking home or loading up their buggies. Their parents had already left an hour before. Susanna was ready to go home, too. She planned to do little but read and relax for the rest of the day. And Amanda? Well, she had plans at the Kaufmann house later that afternoon.

"Where is Traci?" Amanda asked. "I need to get home and work on my sewing before it's time to go to Dale's."

"I don't know," Susanna answered as she scanned the thinning crowd. "She was here. Let's go look in the barns."

Amanda groaned. "How many times have we done this over the years?"

"A lot."

Indeed they had. From the time they were about ten or eleven, it had been their job to track down Traci and get her where she needed to be. Traci was by far the most outgoing of the three sisters. She was also the hardest to get places. Susanna and Amanda had learned over the years to stick together when searching for her in gatherings like this. Otherwise, their little sister would beg and plead with each of them separately to stay just ten minutes longer over and over again.

When they found her at last, standing in the center of about six boys and girls, Susanna smiled. "Look at her. She has already made a lot of friends."

"That's Traci. She never met a group of people she couldn't relate to."

That was true. While Amanda was friendly but sometimes a little tentative, and Susanna was socially awkward, Traci got the best traits of both of their parents. She could talk to anyone, was easy to get along with, and rarely got ruffled.

When they approached, Traci paused midsentence. "Hold on," she told the boy she was speaking to as she crossed the lawn. "You don't want to leave now, do you?"

"Mamm and Daed already left. It is time."

"It's only two. Can't I stay here a while longer?"

"I don't feel right about you getting home by yourself," Amanda said.

"I can walk her back," a dark-haired boy about her age said as he approached. "I don't mind."

"Please?" Traci asked. "This is Hank. Remember, I told you about him after church? His father is one of the preachers."

Sharing a look with Amanda, Susanna shrugged. "I don't see what harm it would be for you to come home later. In an hour or two?"

Traci hugged her. *"Danke."*

Sharing a smile, she and Amanda waved good-bye, then started walking.

"That was sweet, wasn't it?"

"Jah. It reminded me of when we used to beg Mamm and Daed to let us stay late after church."

"I'm glad we let her stay."

Susanna nodded. "I wasn't up for another argument. Plus, she is getting older. When I was her age, Mamm and Daed had me looking after her all the time."

"I was just thinking that," Amanda said. "Hey, Sue?"

"Hmm?"

"Things seem better. Don't you think?"

"Definitely. I think we are finally making friends. It just takes time, I guess." Smiling at her sister, Susanna said, "Of course, who would have expected you and Dale to hit it off so well?"

Amanda flushed. "We haven't 'hit it off.' We just seem to get along well."

"I'm glad for you. That's wonderful."

"I hope so. I want to continue to feel like this. Like everything is going to be just fine here."

Three hours later, Susanna and Amanda were wishing they'd done anything but say yes to Traci.

"I don't understand how you two could have done something so irresponsible," their mother said as she stood on the front porch and scanned the area. "You didn't even know the boy's name."

Amanda flushed. "She did say he was Hank and that she thought he was the son of one of the preachers."

"There are three preachers, Amanda. And furthermore, though I'm not saying the preachers aren't good men, their profession doesn't mean their children don't ever make foolish choices from time to time."

"You're right, Mamm," Amanda said. "I'm sorry."

Mamm folded her arms across her chest. "That don't mean a whole lot right now."

Susanna winced but said nothing. How could she? It was the truth. Traci still wasn't home, and she and Amanda had no information about who she could be with or where she could be.

"We were just trying to be like you, Mamm," Amanda said. "You always used to let us stay late after church."

"That was different. Back in Berlin, you knew everyone around. I did, too. We don't really know the people here."

Susanna couldn't argue with that. "Maybe I should go look for her."

"Where would you look? Your father is already out searching for her. If you go, too, then I'll have three of you to worry about."

Wrapping her arms around her waist, Susanna nodded. She agreed, but it was a terrible thing to feel so hopeless and helpless.

"I bet she just lost track of time," Amanda said hesitantly from behind them. "Traci never thinks about things like that."

"I hope that's the case," Mamm said, her voice thick with worry.

Just then, they saw Traci and their father approaching in the distance. Tears pricked Susanna's eyes, she was so relieved. "There they are. Oh, thank the good Lord. Daed found her."

"I bet he's been lecturing her the whole way home," Amanda said.

"*Nee*," Mamm said slowly. "He's not lecturing her. Look. He's trying to help her walk."

Looking closer, Susanna saw that her father had an arm braced around Traci. It was obvious that he was close to carrying her.

"She looks to be soaking wet!" Mamm cried.

Susanna and Amanda took off running. The closer they got, the higher their anxiety rose.

Traci's face was tearstained and her cheeks were bright red. She was also limping. Her dress looked wet and she was holding her hand in an awkward way.

Susanna got there first. "Traci?" she called out in a rush. "What in the world happened to you? Did you fall into the creek?"

"I didn't fall," she said.

Amanda rushed to join them. "I don't understand. If you didn't fall, how did you get so wet?"

Lips pressed together, Daed shook his head. "That's enough, girls," he said, his voice hard. "We'll talk about this when we get inside. Now, one of you give her your cloak, if you please."

Amanda pulled off her new black cloak and draped it around Traci's shoulders. "There you go."

"Where's your coat, Daed?" Susanna asked.

"Never mind that. We'll talk inside, child. Now help me." Looking over her shoulder, Daed spoke to Amanda. "Hurry back and tell your mother to run a bath and heat up a kettle. We're going to have to get her warm as fast as possible."

With a nod, Amanda rushed back toward the house.

While Amanda ran, Susanna quickly moved to Traci's other side and wrapped an arm around her. She shivered and snuggled closer. "When we get you home, we'll put you in that warm bathtub," she said. "I'll even ask Mamm to let you use some of her special bubble bath."

But even the promise of their mother's favorite lavender-scented bubble bath didn't seem to make a difference in her sister's demeanor. Traci didn't speak another word, she just continued to look at the ground and concentrate on walking.

And their father? Well, he looked shell-shocked. When Traci stumbled, he lifted her into his arms.

When they got to the front steps, her mother rushed forward. "Traci! Traci, I've been so worried. John, is she okay?"

"Hope so," he said as he set Traci down. "Susanna?"

"Yes, Daed. I'm on it. Come on, Traci. Mamm, is the tub running?"

"Amanda started it a couple of seconds ago."

"*Gut*. I'll take her there right now."

"I'll be right there to help you," Mamm said.

"*Nee*, Mamm," Traci said. "I'll be fine."

"But—"

Traci cut her off. "Susanna and Amanda can help me get undressed."

"Oh. All right, then. Now, John, you are going to catch your death."

"I'll be all right. But you shouldn't have gone outside, Leah."

Their voices faded as they headed to their bedroom. Practically carrying her little sister now, Susanna brought her into the bathroom and shut the door.

Amanda had already poured some of their mother's bubble bath into the water. The room was warm and humid and smelled like lavender.

Amanda turned Traci to face her and started unpinning her dress. Needing to do something, Susanna knelt on the ground and unlaced Traci's boots, then helped her out of them. The whole time, their sister was shivering. Traci, her hands fisted, stood still like a statue, trembling from head to toe.

At last, they had her in the tub.

As she continued to shiver, Amanda helped her lean back in the hot soapy water. Soon, she was covered up by bubbles and had gained some color in her face.

When her eyes didn't look so glassy, Susanna knelt on the floor. "Traci, what happened?"

"I was walking home from Hank's. He walked me halfway. All I had to do was go through that patch of woods and over that little bridge over the creek. You know the one we found the first week here, between our house and the Kaufmanns'?"

"I do."

"When I got about halfway, the wood under me broke and I went straight into the water. It was so cold."

"I thought it was iced over," Amanda said.

"I went right through the ice," Traci said, her voice tremulous. "I didn't go under or anything, it wasn't that deep, but I was soaked. When I tried to pull myself out, my skirt got caught. And I injured my hand and foot when I fell, too." She held out her hand.

Susanna gently folded it in between both of hers. It was already bruised and swollen, but it looked more banged up than seriously injured. "I bet it hurts something awful."

"I don't even know anymore. I was so cold and I couldn't get out, then when I finally did, I could hardly walk. And there was no one around. Then I started calling out for help."

"And Daed came at last," said Amanda.

"*Jah*. At last."

Amanda smiled at her sweetly. "It's over now, though. *Jah*? After you get out, you can put on one of my thick flannel nightgowns. Then we'll get you some hot tea and soup or something. I bet Daed already has a new fire going."

Traci nodded but the troubled look in her eyes still remained.

"What is it?" Susanna asked.

"Th . . . There was something wrong with that board."

"I'm sure it was rotten or something," Amanda said soothingly.

"*Nee*. It snapped in half. Mandy, Sue, don'tcha remember when we went exploring? All three of us stood on that bridge at the same time. It was strong. It was really strong."

Susanna exchanged a worried glance with Amanda. "Traci, what are you saying?" she asked at last.

"I'm saying that this wasn't an accident. Someone messed with that board. They wanted one of us to fall in."

A chill ran through her as she stared at her little sister. Traci was crying now.

"Sue, Mandy, you've gotta believe me," she said, sounding frantic. "Someone weakened that board on purpose! I know it. I know it! Someone wanted one of us to get hurt."

Sitting back on her heels, Susanna met Amanda's gaze.

In her eyes, Susanna saw a reflection of what she was feeling. Amanda wasn't afraid that Traci was lying. She feared that she was telling the truth.

CHAPTER 11

Sunday Night, December 17

Once Traci calmed down, finally sinking deeper into the hot water and soothing bubbles, Susanna got to her feet.

"We're going to get out of here and let you soak in privacy for a little while. Is that okay?"

Traci nodded. "Does that mean that you believe me?"

"I think you've given us a lot to think about," Susanna hedged. Traci needed to be soothed and calmed down, not agitated further.

"Tomorrow, when I'm better, we'll go over there and I'll show you," Traci promised. "Or maybe Daed can take you out there tonight."

"I have a feeling Daed isn't going to want to do anything but recover," Amanda said gently. "We were really worried about you, Traci."

"But this is important. I wouldn't lie."

"I don't think you're lying," Susanna said as she edged to the door.

Looking even more upset, Traci bit her bottom lip. "What about you, Mandy?"

"Of course I believe you," Amanda said quickly.

Traci stared at Susanna. "What if your buggy accident hadn't been just an accident? What if someone had been meaning to hurt you?"

She swallowed. "And now someone is sabotaging our bridge? It makes sense . . . except that all we did was buy a farm that was for sale."

Amanda walked to the door. "Little sister, please. Calm yourself. I don't want you to get sick. Now, I'm going to go make sure you have something warm for when you get out."

Traci nodded slowly. "All right."

After she and Amanda left the bathroom, Susanna sighed. She hated to admit it, but Traci had a point. "Do you think she could be right?" she asked quietly.

Amanda shrugged. "I don't see how she could be."

"But what if these things are all connected? Don't forget, our fence was broken, too."

"That fence was also the Kaufmanns'."

"I don't think they were a target."

"We haven't done anything wrong," Amanda said with more force. "The only reason people are paying any attention is because we're new here to town. We can't start letting our imaginations run away with us."

That did make sense. She wanted it to. "Let's go talk to Mamm and Daed. Maybe Daed got a better idea of what happened than Traci."

After Amanda pulled out one of her soft flannel nightgowns for Traci, they walked into the kitchen. Their parents were sitting at the kitchen table. Mamm was drinking hot apple cider while Daed was sipping hot chicken soup. He already had put on fresh clothes, including a thick pair of socks that Amanda had knitted for him last year for Christmas.

Pausing for a moment, Susanna not only gave thanks that they were home safe but that they were now all together every night. She needed to keep focused on what a blessing that was.

While Amanda went right in and hugged their father, Susanna took a moment to appreciate the scene in front of her. They were not only all together, they were sitting at their kitchen table, which in a lot of ways had become the cornerstone of their family.

It almost hadn't made the move to Kentucky. Daed had been so happy to be finally giving them a lovely new, big home, with a big kitchen, that he wanted to celebrate the move by purchasing a new table, one that would be suitable for their new surroundings. Susanna and her sisters had all thought that was a good idea.

The table was old, had a crack down the center of it, and was really too small for five people. It also brought back a lot of memories of just the four of them sitting around it while Daed was gone for the week, working for Mr. Fowler.

Getting a new table that was big enough for all of them to sit together seemed like a wonderful idea.

But it had been their mother who had resisted. She hadn't wanted to spend the money . . . or give up the memories that it brought her.

And because their father could never tell their mother no, they'd put it in the moving van.

Now Susanna was so grateful for it. Ever since they'd

moved, they'd had a lot of trouble and worry. That table symbolized security for her.

Mamm looked up when Susanna finally sat and joined them. "How is she?"

"She looks better," Susanna said. "She has some color in her cheeks. I told her to soak for a bit."

"We put in some of your bubble bath, Mamm," Amanda added.

"Good. I hope it relaxes her." Rubbing her temples, she said, "What a night. Until we saw your father holding her the way he was, it never crossed my mind that Traci had been hurt. I just thought she'd forgotten the time."

"Me, too," Susanna said.

After pouring herself a cup of tea, Amanda sat next to their father. "Daed, Traci said something kind of disturbing. She said that one of the boards of the bridge had been damaged. Maybe even on purpose."

He frowned. "She mentioned that to me, too."

"What do you think? Could she be right? Did you see anything?"

"It was too dark to tell." He shrugged. "I told her that was probably not the case, though."

There was something in the way he spoke that gave her pause. "Do you think there could be a reason someone might want to do that?"

"I don't want there to be . . ." After he took a fortifying sip of tea, he added, "But it is disconcerting, especially coming so close to that fence being broken the way it was."

"So you think it's a possibility," Susanna said.

"*Nee*, I didn't say that." Looking at her intently, he added, "Sue, we are trying to make a new life for ourselves here. We want to be a part of the community. A positive part of the community. No one is going to appreciate us making a big fuss about a couple of weak boards in an old bridge."

Mamm nodded. "People are finally realizing that the Vances' financial troubles had nothing to do with us, too. And we have a whole farm to manage now. That's too much on our plate to be making up problems where they don't exist."

Susanna heard what her parents were saying, but didn't necessarily agree that they all should be sticking their heads in the sand. "But we can't forget that many things have been happening to us that are out of the ordinary. Why, since we've moved here, we've had my buggy accident, then the fence, and now this. It can't just be a string of unfortunate events."

"It might be," Mamm said. "I think this is just a case of Traci letting her imagination get the best of her."

After looking over her shoulder to make sure Traci wasn't walking their way, Susanna added, "I'm going to go look at that bridge just to make sure."

"I'm not going to stop you, Susanna," Daed said after sharing a look with their mother. "But please watch who you talk to about this. Don't go starting trouble where there is none."

"I won't say anything to anyone else. But I do think we need to check the board for Traci. Just to be sure."

"You going to play detective, Sue?" Amanda teased.

"*Nee*. Well, maybe." She yearned to laugh, and make light of her suspicions, but she simply wasn't able to do that. She still had nightmares about her buggy accident. She also believed Traci. Their little sister was a lot of things, but she wasn't the type of girl to make up stories about broken boards.

"Please, be careful," Amanda whispered.

"Don't worry. I intend to be." Actually, it would make her extremely happy to walk out to the bridge, see a couple of rotten boards, and realize that her little sister had simply had a bad accident.

She hoped and prayed that was the case.

CHAPTER 12

Monday, December 18

It had been a long day. An endless one. Neil had put in ten long hours at Horse Cave Salvage, much of it in the back of a warehouse in shipping and receiving. Because they received cartons of food and medicines close to their expiration dates from all over the area, the loading dock was always busy. Usually, he liked how fast the hours flew by. But sometimes, such as that afternoon, he found himself wishing that Horse Cave Salvage wasn't as popular a store as it was.

By the time he'd clocked out, his arms felt like they were about to fall off from unloading freight from a semi that had arrived at six in the morning.

Most drivers stepped in to give folks a hand, but not that one. After informing them all that he was union and paid to drive freight, not load or unload it, he'd sat down with his phone and either played games on it or aimlessly watched Neil; his manager, Junior; and two other men unload and restack boxes for two hours.

Then, after the driver left, they'd had to rearrange everything yet again, thanks to an unexpected delivery that had arrived two days early.

By the time Junior had waved him off at four, Neil was in a terrible mood and only wanted some time to himself. Not even the envelope holding his sizable paycheck lifted his spirits.

Keeping his head down, he strode through the crowded store, hoping to avoid having to speak to anyone he knew. When he at last stepped outside and breathed deep, he was struck by how much the weather had changed since they'd closed the warehouse doors. It was bitterly cold and spitting snow. As his body struggled to adjust to the sudden change in temperature, he burrowed his head and shoulders further into his coat.

It seemed to be a fitting end to his workday. Because they'd sold their horse and buggy, he was reduced to walking home from work. Though Neil could easily call for a driver, even the thought of standing around at his place of work for another fifteen minutes was unacceptable.

Lengthening his stride, he concentrated on hurrying home and ignoring the people he passed in the parking lot. He didn't want to help any customers, and he really didn't want to chat with anyone he knew.

Then he saw her.

Susanna Schwartz was loading four or five cases of large Mason jars in the back of her buggy. Her expression was strained as she wrapped her hands around a case and hefted it.

He wanted to walk by. He knew if he did, she would probably never even know that he'd ignored her.

But he couldn't do that. Not again, at least. Dale had been

right the other day when they'd been standing in the middle of his snowy field. Neil's circumstances might have changed, but he had not. No matter what happened in his life, he wasn't the type of man to watch a woman struggle by herself.

Especially not her.

Mentally preparing himself to take part in yet another awkward conversation, Neil walked to Susanna's side. "Hiya," he said simply.

She stilled. "Neil. Hello. What are you doing here?"

"At the moment, I'm trying to help you," he said as he shooed her hands away. When she stared at him in confusion, he lifted one of the heavy cases and placed it in her buggy.

After a pause, she stepped away. "*Danke.* Those boxes were heavier than they looked."

"They always are."

Humor, and a new burst of awareness, filled her eyes. "Sounds like you've lifted your share of boxes."

"Only today." Though his arms protested, he picked up the last two cases together and deposited them in the back of the buggy. Tried to tell himself that he had not just done that to show how strong he was. "I unloaded freight for hours today."

"You work here?"

"*Jah.*"

A new line of worry marred her forehead. "Do you hate it?"

He realized she was feeling guilty about their situation. "You know what? I don't. It turns out I enjoy getting off the land, working an honest day's work, and getting paid for it, too. Today just happened to be a long day."

"I've had a long Monday, too. I had meant to do something

important this morning, but I couldn't get out of the house until now. I finally decided to work on these."

Glad to be concentrating on her instead of himself, he tapped one of the boxes. "What are you going to do with all of these?"

She smiled brightly. It transformed her features from pleasing to beautiful. "Oh! They are Christmas gifts."

Smiling right back at her, he couldn't resist teasing. "So, you're going to be giving out Mason jars for Christmas?"

"Ha, ha." Pointing to the large bags of beans and rice that were already in the buggy, she said, "I'm making soup mix. I'll layer on the dried peas, white beans, and other ingredients in the jar, then attach a recipe to it with a red-and-green ribbon."

He'd seen things like that in fancy gift shops. "I bet it will look real nice."

"I hope so. I'm going to try my best."

"Looks like you're making a lot of it." He was kind of surprised. He hadn't thought she knew too many people well yet, but maybe he simply didn't understand women and gift giving.

She chuckled. "You're right. I am. Some are gifts, but I am going to try to sell some, too. When I went in Blooms and Berries the other day to get some garland, I noticed that they sold a lot of items like this. Waneta, the woman who was working, said tourists come in to get Amish-made crafts. I thought I would make some to sell for some extra money."

She'd surprised him. He'd been so fixated on his family's losses and her family's gains that it hadn't occurred to him that she was also feeling the pinch of the holiday season. "I hope it is successful."

"Me, too."

With the last cases well situated in the back, Neil closed the buggy and moved her shopping cart to the corral. She stood to one side, watching him.

He realized then that she was wearing a thick wool dress in a dark-evergreen fabric. Over it, she had a traditional black cloak. Black knit gloves were on her hands, and she was wearing a black bonnet over her *kapp*. Her light-brown hair, fair complexion, and green eyes stood out against the dark colors.

She really *was* pretty. But there was something else about her that he admired, too. He liked how assertive she was. He liked that she was trying to help her family.

Most of all, he was glad that she seemed as hopeful as he did that they were putting their first awkward conversation to rest. When he realized that he'd been standing next to the line of metal shopping carts, staring at her while lost in thought, he knew it was time to go.

"Well, I'll be seeing you. Good luck with your soup mix."

"*Danke*. And thank you for your help, too. If you hadn't stopped, I would still be trying to get those jars into the buggy."

"You would have done it. I'm starting to think that you just might do anything you set out to do."

"I don't know about that, but I'm willing to try. That's all one can do."

"Indeed. Well, good-bye."

Her smile dimmed. "Wait! Are you walking home now?"

"*Jah*. Like I said, I just finished my shift. And with the snow? It's time I got home. You, too."

"My word. You worked all day, helped me with my cart, and now are walking home. Would you like a ride?"

"It's out of your way."

"I don't have anything else to do this afternoon. I would enjoy the drive."

He knew he shouldn't accept her offer. Though he believed her family wasn't the reason for his family's living situation, his father wasn't of the same mind. However, his legs were tired, his body was aching for a break, and his arms were just as worn out. "All right, then. I accept."

AS SUSANNA CLICKED the reins and coaxed Midge forward, she could hardly believe that Neil Vance had accepted her offer of a ride. She also was pretty surprised that he'd stopped to help her. She'd been caught off guard about how warm and friendly he'd been acting, too.

Obviously, she still had a lot to learn about Neil. He was more complex than she'd first imagined.

She was also becoming attracted to him. With the side doors of the buggy shut tightly against the cold, he seemed to take up the majority of the small space.

Or maybe she just couldn't seem to think of anything but him.

Maybe it was because he was so different than most any other man she'd been so close to. He was big. Big hands, broad shoulders, barrel chested.

His voice was as deep as she remembered, too. She also liked how he didn't play games with her. Before, he hadn't liked her. Then, he asked her to forgive him.

Now it did seem they were becoming friends.

"Guess what? We had quite a scare last night. My little sister Traci fell into the creek."

"What? Which one?"

"The one dividing the Kaufmanns' property from ours." She paused, unsure if she'd just put her foot in her mouth.

But instead of looking hurt, he merely stared at her curiously. "Did she slip on the rocks? Is she hurt?"

"One of the boards broke on the bridge. She fell onto the ice and it broke. But she's okay." Thinking of Traci's stuffy nose and small fever in the morning, she amended her words. "Well, for the most part. I think that accident gave her a cold."

"It's a blessing she didn't get hurt worse."

"I agree." For a moment, Susanna considered telling him about how Traci was sure someone had sabotaged the boards, then decided to keep that information to herself. They were finally getting along; no need for her to make things awkward again.

"Please tell her that I hope she feels better soon."

"*Danke*. I will." They drew to a stop at an intersection. The snow had lessened. Since they were on a back road, no cars were around. It was just the two of them for miles. "Where to now?" she asked.

"Turn right. We're going to go about two miles down the road, then you can drop me off."

"At your house?"

"*Nee*. I think it would be best if I got out at the front gate. There's a good place to turn around there, too."

"I'll stop wherever you ask, but . . . is it also that you don't want your family to see us together?"

She could practically feel the tension between them return. "Partly. My father might not understand."

"What about your brother and mother? Do they dislike me also?"

"Nee." Staring straight ahead, he murmured, "Susanna, this problem lies with my father and his disappointments with himself, not you."

"I'm so glad you don't hate me."

"I never hated you. I was upset with the situation. I was ashamed that everyone I knew was aware of my family's problems. I took some of that embarrassment and anger out on you and I'm sorry about that."

"I understand."

He looked at her again. This time there was a sweet tenderness in his gaze. "I hope so, Susanna. I want us to be friends. I also really, really hope we can start having conversations that don't feel like minefields."

"Me, too. Hey, have you talked to Dale lately?"

"Only briefly at church. Why?"

"I was just wondering if he told you that my family visited his a couple of days ago."

"I'm glad they invited you over."

"They didn't. You see, my father discovered that someone damaged our fence. Daed wanted to ask if they knew anything about it. My mother decided that we should all go. She even had us bring a pie."

"What do you mean, someone damaged the fence? What happened?"

"It was on the north side of the property. Near the grove of pecan trees. A good six-foot section was torn off and in pieces on the ground."

"I've never heard of something like that happening before."

"I think the Kaufmanns were taken aback about it at first. I think Mr. Kaufmann thought my father was even accusing them. But of course my *daed* said that he couldn't imagine anyone wanting to do so much damage to their own fencing."

"Did the Kaufmanns have any idea of what could have happened?"

"*Nee.* I think everyone's hoping it was just some random act of violence."

"That doesn't make sense," he murmured before he pointed to the entrance to a large farm with an impressive front gate. "You can let me off here."

Carefully, she directed Midge to the side of the road. Hoping to end their conversation on a lighter note, she cleared her throat. "Something else happened during our visit to the Kaufmanns."

"Oh? And what was that?"

"Dale took my sister Amanda outside to visit privately."

Neil's posture relaxed as he smiled broadly. "Somehow I ain't too surprised about that."

"I wasn't, either. Between you and me, I think my sister really likes Dale."

"I can't wait to ask him about that."

"Um, try not to make it sound like I was gossiping about him."

"I know you weren't. We were merely catching up on news. That's all." Then, to her surprise, he reached out and took hold of her hand. It felt rough and warm against her bare skin. Almost comforting. "Thank you for giving me a ride home. Be careful driving back to your house, okay? The roads can be slick."

"I will," she whispered.

After giving her hand a small, gentle squeeze, he climbed out of the buggy. "I'll be seeing you, Susanna."

She smiled at his comment. But as she watched him walk away, Susanna wondered what exactly he meant. Did she simply imagine he'd see her around town? Or did he have something different in mind?

CHAPTER 13

Monday, December 18

I didn't expect you to be home at this time of day," Neil's father said when he walked into the house. "Why aren't you at work? Did you call off early?"

And just like that, all of the warm thoughts he'd been entertaining about Susanna evaporated. In some ways, his comment was more jarring to his insides than that first burst of cold air had been to his cheeks that afternoon.

"Of course not, Daed. I worked a full day." More than that, actually. "I was fortunate to get a ride home."

"With whom?"

"No one you know," he said, hating to fib but taking comfort in the fact that he wasn't actually lying. "Where are Mamm and Roy?"

Your mother is over with Joseph. He asked for her help with his laundry. Roy is still at his new job."

"Still? He went into work earlier than I did."

"He said the Costa family is paying him a lot of overtime

right now. I'm glad he's taking advantage of that. He needs to earn his keep."

His father's criticism and harsh tone were new and difficult to get used to. Ever since he'd told all of them about his many financial mistakes, he acted like a different man. Now he seemed to find fault with all of them. Nearly every conversation with him was filled with complaints and jabs.

He didn't use to act that way. When Neil was little, he remembered his father always being patient with him. He'd never raised his voice when a glass broke or he'd done poorly on a paper or test at school.

He'd been even more understanding with Roy, often chuckling when his little brother had messed up a chore.

Neil supposed his father had good reason for his shift in attitude. Uncle Joe had made his life very difficult. And now that they were all living on the same property and his father essentially worked for him, his father never got a break from him.

So, yes, his father's dissatisfaction with his life was understandable. But his sniping made a tough living situation even worse.

"How was your day, Daed?"

Sipping his glass of water, he shrugged. "About how you would expect. Joe asked me to work in the tack room today, mending lines and oiling bridles."

"At least you were inside."

His father rolled his eyes. "It was a waste of time. Everything in there was already in good order. I had told Joe that we needed to order seeds and such for spring planting, but he thinks it's too early."

"It's December."

"I know. By this time, we not only usually have everything ordered, but most of it has been delivered and organized in the barn."

"What did he do while you were in the tack room?"

"Who knows? He wasn't around me. That's all I cared about."

"I feel badly that Mamm is at his house doing laundry. She already does so much around here. She shouldn't have to take on more work, too."

"I know, but she said it wasn't a problem."

Neil knew that she most likely was trying to keep everyone happy. That was his mother's way. Standing up, he pulled the paycheck from his pocket. "I got paid today. Here you go, Daed."

For the first time since he got home, his father's expression became less caustic and far more vulnerable. "You know, Neil, I think you should start keeping your pay. We have money in the bank now; and though Joe is a thorn in my side, he does pay me well."

"How about I help contribute for a little while longer? Christmas is coming up, you know."

"I doubt we'll be celebrating this year, Neil."

"I know we won't be exchanging gifts or anything, but give the money to Mamm. She can use it to buy a turkey. Or all of her baking supplies. You know how she likes to give all those cookie tins to practically everyone she's ever met."

"This ain't the year for her to do that."

"You know how much she likes baking all those cookies. We can't tell her no."

His father laughed, the noise sounding harsh and brittle in the cramped room. "Of course I can. It would be too awkward, anyway. Now everyone who we give those tins to will know how bad our situation has become."

Usually, Neil would back down. But they'd already been through so much. There was no way he wasn't going to fight for one of his mother's favorite activities of the whole year. "She loves making those gifts, Daed. She writes everyone notes. And it doesn't matter where we live, anyway. It's still Christmas."

"You are acting as if what we've just been through doesn't matter."

"*Nee*, I'm acting as if us living in this house on Uncle Joseph's property isn't the end of the world. We still have each other, Daed. We're still getting up every morning. We can't simply hide out here until things change."

"You watch your mouth, boy."

Neil gritted his teeth but held his temper. "Yes, sir."

The door opened then, bringing in a burst of cold air, his mother, and Roy.

"Oh good, you're here!" Roy called out as he shifted a large paper sack in his arms. "Now you can hear the story Mamm was telling me about Joseph's laundry room. You'll never believe this—he keeps a turtle in there!"

"It's the sweetest thing, really," Mamm began as she glanced at Neil and his father. Her smile faded. "What's wrong?"

But instead of answering, Daed surged to his feet. "What is that, Roy? You are supposed to be working, not going out and spending money. Has this year not taught you anything?"

Roy carefully set the bag on the counter. "This is a gift from Mr. and Mrs. Costa." Pausing dramatically, he said, "I've been noticing that Mr. Costa is having a time of it, looking after his wife and their two little girls and all. So the other day I asked him if I could start staying a little later so he could be with his wife."

"Mrs. Costa is expecting again," Mamm said. "You men probably wouldn't have heard about that."

Roy nodded. "He was so pleased when I was about ready to leave, he gave me this sack full of food."

"He gave you food?" Daed asked.

"Well, *jah*." Warily, Roy glanced at Neil, then at their mother.

Her smile now forced, Mamm said, "I think it's so cute how Jonathan Costa dotes on his *frau*. He acts like she's made of glass and is always fussing over her. I'm real glad that our Roy has been so helpful to them, too. Even though they're Englishers, they're some of my favorite people in the county."

"*Jah*, what you offered, that was real good," Neil said as their father continued to stew. "I'm sure they appreciated your kindness."

Roy smiled. "*Danke*. I was nervous about overstepping myself, but Mr. Costa told me he was so pleased that he'd hired me to help with the livestock and the extra chores around the farm." Pointing to the paper sack, he said, "That's why he gave me this sack. I think he knew I wouldn't have wanted extra money. He told me that those cans and things were just sitting around, but I have a feeling that they bought them especially for us." Reaching into a sack, he pulled out a roasted chicken. "He even gave us a chicken," he said with a laugh. "He said Mrs. Costa roasted two chickens too many when their relatives came over."

"Now I'll hardly have to cook tonight at all," Mamm said, her eyes shining.

"We canna accept it," Daed said.

Roy carefully put the chicken down on the counter. "Why not?"

"It's charity. No one gives food unless they think the receivers can't afford to buy their own. And we can."

"I can't take the food back to them, Daed," Roy said. "It would be rude."

"It was rude of him to give it to you in the first place."

"He meant well. It wasn't rude. And it wasn't charity, either. Why, you know how important Mr. Costa is. He's a part owner in several businesses all over the county. All he wanted to do was give us something, the same way Mamm makes everyone cookies each Christmas."

"It ain't the same." Pointing to the door, he said, "Go take that food back right now."

"*Nee*," Roy said, his tone full of ice. "I'm not going to disrespect Mr. and Mrs. Costa like that."

"But you'll disrespect me?"

"If doing the right thing means disrespecting you, then yeah, I guess I am."

Just as their father inhaled, Neil pressed a hand on his brother's shoulder. "Go take a shower or something," he said quietly. "I'll deal with this."

Roy shook his head. "*Nee, bruder.* It ain't like that anymore. I'm not going to run off while you attempt to fix things." Glaring at their father, he said, "It's time you stopped feeling sorry for yourself, Daed."

"You are talking nonsense."

"You deliberately twisted and turned a kindness into something ugly. What is more, you've been doing things like this for some time now. It needs to stop."

Twin spots of color appeared on their father's cheeks.

"You have forgotten who you are speaking to, Roy. I raised you better than this."

"*Nee*, you raised me to respect others, have faith in Jesus, and practice forgiveness toward others. I can't say that you've exhibited any of those behaviors lately."

"Roy," Mamm whispered. "You must stop."

As their father clenched his fists and visibly attempted to rein in his temper, Roy shook his head. "No, Mamm. I ain't going to sit here and watch Neil work long hours, watch you try to pretend that we're all okay, and keep my mouth shut while my father bites at all of us just because he wishes we still had our farm. He needs to come to terms with the fact that we don't have it . . . but we are still okay."

Walking across the small space, Roy clasped one of his father's arms. "Daed, *we are still okay*. Stop grieving for what we lost and, if you can, learn to be grateful for what we still have."

"Unhand me, boy."

Immediately, Roy dropped his hand. After a long minute, he exhaled and turned away.

Neil felt tears in his eyes as he watched Roy walk down the hall to the shower, his mother press her palms to her cheeks, and his father walk out the door.

Feeling like the weight of the world was on his shoulders, Neil sat back down, closed his eyes, and prayed for them all.

CHAPTER 14

Tuesday, December 19

Tuesday morning dawned bright and sunny. Susanna was grateful for the good weather since the mood inside their house was rather dark.

When she'd awoken, she'd discovered Amanda sitting next to Traci on the couch with her arms wrapped around her. Traci was pale. Her eyes were watering and she had a terrible cough.

Then their mother informed her that Daed was just as sick and was in bed. After helping with some chores around the house, and realizing that the rest of the inhabitants in the house were about to take naps, Susanna decided to finally go out to the bridge and try to figure out what had happened.

She needed to prove Traci wrong. She needed to be able to tell herself that no one could have tried to damage the bridge on purpose.

She set off, determined to spend some time appreciating how beautiful everything looked all covered in white.

She also used the time to try to reflect on how she was feeling. She thought back to before they moved to Horse Cave. She'd been so excited and hopeful when their father had first told them about his inheritance and his bid on this farm.

It hadn't even occurred to her then to think about the family that was selling the farm. Now that she'd met Neil Vance, though, she was wondering why the Lord had put them on either side of such contrasting beliefs.

Approaching the bridge, she noticed the broken board right away. It was split in two. Below it, the five-foot-wide creek was frozen . . . with the exception of a sizable hole in the ice.

Staring at it, she imagined Traci falling through the ice, being scared, at a loss for what to do. The only saving grace was that it wasn't terribly deep. The water was only about three and a half feet deep. Not enough for a thirteen-year-old girl to drown in . . . unless she'd hit her head and gotten trapped under the ice.

A chill that had nothing to do with the cold temperatures settled inside her. Traci could have died.

After allowing herself a few seconds of grief, she shook it off and got back to the reason she'd come there. She needed to inspect the boards, to see if there was any visible mark or indication that could prove Traci's suspicion correct.

She stepped toward the bridge, suddenly wishing that she hadn't come alone. Of course, even if she did fall through another board, she would be okay. She wasn't a scared teenager, she was taller than Traci, and it was a bright day. She wasn't going to get stuck or disoriented or overcome by panic.

But it still would have been better to have gone with another person.

After eyeing the wood slats as well as she could from the bank, she knew she had only one option if she was going to hope to find any answers. She was going to need to get on the bridge, kneel down on one of the sturdier planks, and then peer at the broken wood.

Decision made, she set down the little quilted backpack she'd been carrying and stepped onto the bridge. Immediately, her foot slid.

It was icy.

Glad she was wearing gloves that had a bit of a grip on them, she clutched the handrail and took another step. Then two more.

She was about two feet in. After another couple of steps, she would be able to kneel down and look for damage.

Feeling more determined, she took another tentative step. The wood groaned under her weight. Had this one been sabotaged, too? Perhaps if she knelt on one knee. Wasn't dispersing her weight supposed to be better in—

"What are you doing?"

Startled, she turned, then felt her foot slide on another patch of ice.

Neil Vance muttered something as he reached out for her and grabbed her by the waist.

"Hey, what are *you* doing?" she asked around a squeal . . . as he brought her off the bridge and set her down on the bank of the creek.

Then, there they were, standing together, his large hands firmly grasping her by her waist. Somehow hers were now on his forearms. Holding on to his thick wool coat.

Once again, she was reminded how tall he was. With his

boots on, he stood at least six inches taller than she. His un-usual flinty-blue eyes studied her expression.

Then promptly set her free.

"What am *I* doing?" he repeated, giving her a look that said that he thought she had completely lost her mind. "I'm trying to save a second Schwartz sister from falling into the creek."

"I wasn't about to fall."

"Well, you really shouldn't have been trying to cross it."

"I wasn't. I was only attempting to get a better idea of what happened."

He looked around. "So you came out here by yourself."

Since that was obvious, Susanna pointed to the hole in the ice instead. "Traci fell in right there. Then her dress got caught on a rock or branch or something in the ice."

"How did she get out?"

"My father found her."

"And she *really* is all right?"

Worry laced his tone. He *was* worried about Traci, and that helped her calm down and act less argumentative. Lift-ing a shoulder, she answered with care. "More or less. As I told you, she's a bit sick, with a bad cold now; and we learned she also turned her ankle. She should be right as rain in a couple of days." Staring at the hole in the ice, she felt an unwanted tremor race down her spine. "She could have been hurt much worse."

"Susanna, if you needed to cross the creek this morning, you should have just walked across on the rocks. It's frozen solid because it's so shallow there."

"Is that what you did?"

"*Jah.*" Looking over her, he said, "Are you scared to cross on the ice? I can help you, if you'd like."

"That's kind of you." It was actually really kind. So far, everything that he'd been doing, lifting her off the bridge, offering to help . . . well, it was all very kind.

It was time to tell him the truth.

"I was hoping to get a good look at the wood planks."

"You can't fix it today, Susanna. Listen, when the weather gets a little warmer, I'll come out here with Roy or Dale and repair it."

"I hate to point out the obvious, but this bridge isn't your problem anymore."

"Don't be so stubborn. I'm trying to help you. Listen, I helped my father build this bridge. Dale and Roy helped repair a couple of loose boards just last summer. We know what we're doing."

"The boards were replaced that recently?"

He paused. "Yes. Why?"

"That just surprises me."

"Because? Wait. What do you want to inspect?"

"To see if the wood had been tampered with." Before he could say something sarcastic, she said, "Traci is sure that someone weakened the board. She heard a sharp snap as it broke."

"Anything that breaks would make a snap, don't you think?"

"Usually, I would agree, but she also pointed out that recently she, Amanda, and I all stood on the bridge at the same time. None of us heard any creaking. The wood seemed strong." Blowing out a burst of air, she said, "And you just said you thought it was in good repair."

He looked wary. "I thought it was. But snow and rain and everything else can weaken it. I bet that is what happened."

"Traci is small. She's only about a hundred pounds, Neil. Maybe even a little less than that."

All traces of humor were gone from his face now. "Why would someone want to tamper with this bridge?"

"I don't know, but I have a guess."

He folded his arms over his chest. "You might as well tell me."

"I think someone wanted one of us to get hurt so we would start to get afraid of living here."

"I think you're letting your imagination get the best of ya. Boards break all the time."

"That is true. But then again, someone did shoot at me just a couple of weeks ago. And then, there was the broken fence."

"Don't you think you are jumping to conclusions?"

"*Nee*. Someone wants us gone and isn't going to rest until that happens." Looking at him directly in the eye, she lifted her chin. "I've decided I'm going to figure out who it is."

CHAPTER 15

Tuesday, December 19

A lot of unexpected things had happened in his life, but Neil couldn't ever remember anyone telling him something so outlandish that it took his breath away.

"Are you serious?" he asked.

She was standing so rigid and stiff. So tightly wound up, he could practically see the tension emanating from her. A breeze blew through, pulling up the edge of her cloak to reveal a bright-blue wool dress. That dress, combined with her robin's-egg-blue knit scarf and matching gloves, made him think of the blue jays that often nested in the woods. So bright and cheerful, yet so wary of everything and everyone around them.

It was hard not to smile at her—both because of her looks, which were so cute, and her words, which were completely ridiculous.

Her green eyes flashed in annoyance. "Of course I'm serious. Why would I ever joke about something like this?"

He was thinking that maybe the question should be more along the lines of why would anyone assume they were being shot at. It was quite a stretch to imagine such a thing. "I'm sure no one was shooting at you, Susanna."

"No, you don't understand. I heard gunshots."

"I'm sure you did," he allowed. "But someone was probably hunting in the woods nearby. I don't know how things were in Ohio, but here, a lot of men go out hunting the day after Thanksgiving. It's tradition."

The muscles in her throat tightened as it became obvious that she was trying to hold her temper. "I know about hunting season, Neil. Actually, I thought it was just some hunters at first. But then the shots were fired closer."

He bet she just thought they sounded that way. "Sometimes, the wind can—"

"*Nee.*" She shook her head. "Someone tried to shoot my buggy. They were aiming for me. On purpose."

She was getting worked up. She really believed it. Though he didn't know her hardly at all, even he could sense that she wasn't the type of girl who enjoyed lots of dramatics.

Deciding to take another approach, he said, "I was right there after you wrecked. I didn't see anyone lurking about." He remembered something then. "I was even kind of surprised that no one came over to check on us. Those hunters had to have been nearby."

Susanna stared at him a moment, obviously searching his face to see if he was being honest or patronizing. Finally, she sighed. "It's okay if you don't believe me. I know what I heard. I know what happened."

"Did you ever talk to the sheriff about that?"

For the first time, doubt filled her eyes. "*Nee.* I feared the officers would do what you are doing now."

"Which is?"

"Trying not to laugh."

That sobered him right up. "I'm sorry. I don't want to make you feel bad, but I do think you might have let your imagination run away with you."

"Neil, like I said before, this isn't really any of your concern. I didn't ask you to meet me here and I really didn't ask you to help me. Why don't you go on your way now."

He couldn't believe how stubborn she was! "You are still going to do your bridge inspection?"

"I came here to do that. Of course I am." She gave him a little sarcastic wave with one gloved hand. "Thank you for your interest, but there's no need to stay. Hope you have a nice day."

There was no way he was going to wander off while she walked and climbed around on a rickety bridge by herself. "I'll help you. Stay here. I'll get on the broken bridge and let you know what I see."

"There is no need, Neil. I can do this." Her chin rose a fraction. "Besides, you may not even know what I am looking for."

His amusement about the situation was fast rolling into exasperation. "I promise that I'll let you know if I see anything fishy."

"Fishy?" Her eyes narrowed. "Is that some kind of pun?"

"*Nee.*" Unable to resist, he winked. "It was a good one, though. *Jah?*"

It looked like it was taking everything she had to fight a reluctant smile. But in the end, the smile won. "Maybe," she said at last.

When their eyes met again, there was something new between them. Not friendship, not exactly. Yet. But it was a new type of connection. A bond. Maybe a new understanding of each other, perhaps?

Or, maybe, just maybe, a hint of attraction lay between them now. With a start, he realized that was what he was feeling. "Susanna, I'm not going to let you get on that bridge."

"If Traci was your little sister, you would do the same thing."

"I agree . . . but I must warn you that you have probably let your imagination get the best of you. Traci likely stepped on a broken board. No one would come on the property to sabotage things. You are probably wrong."

Just like he'd set a match, her temper flared. "Don't you understand, Neil? That is the point! I want to be wrong. I don't want someone to hurt me or my sisters. All my family wanted to do when we moved out here was have what we'd always dreamed of having. A farm. Space. Rooms of our own. But everyone seems to think that was sinful of us."

"It wasn't sinful."

She continued as if he hadn't spoken. "Now things are happening that feel deliberate. If someone is targeting us, wanting us to leave, I need to know."

"I understand."

"Do you? My little sister could have really been hurt. I can't ignore that. I don't want it to happen again. That is why I have to check."

Everything she said made sense. He wondered if she could be right. And, he wondered if his family's attitude had encouraged others to go out of their way to hurt the Schwartz family. Had their selfishness and pity party encouraged others to deliberately hurt them?

"You know what? I'm sorry for arguing with you. You are right. If I had a family member who said she thought there was something suspicious about the board breaking, I would have come out here, too. It's also your right. It's your bridge."

She exhaled. "All right, then."

"Let me go, though. You stand on the side. I promise I'll look carefully."

At last she nodded.

Feeling like he'd just won a battle he hadn't planned on fighting, he got on the bridge.

"Careful. It's icy!" she warned, though she knew she sounded like a fool.

He ignored her and decided to get on his knees so he could look at the boards from close up.

He'd been on this bridge hundreds of times. When he'd been a little boy, he'd played pirate ship and all kinds of things on it. Later, he'd helped rebuild it. Then, of course, there were all the times he'd run over it full tilt, trying to get home in time for supper.

As he slowly crawled his way toward the center, he heard unfamiliar creaking and groaning. The boards were giving under his weight. Protesting it.

That had never happened before.

He stopped when he was close to the broken board. Taking care to keep as much of his weight on the other boards, he leaned closer. Took hold of the board that was broken in half. One half had fallen into the creek. But this side?

He had a clear view of how it had been broken.

He ran a finger over the break. Firmly anticipating seeing

that it would be all splintered. But instead, about half of it had been sawed through.

Sawed.

Susanna was right. Someone had intended for a member of the Schwartz family to fall. Maybe to get hurt.

A knot formed in his stomach as he started imagining who could have done such a thing.

CHAPTER 16

Tuesday, December 19

Neil Vance's countenance was far different when he hopped off the bridge and faced her. Just minutes before, his expression had been filled with doubt and maybe even a little bit of humor. Now a new seriousness gleamed in his light-blue eyes.

"You are right," he said simply.

Her spine prickled as dread filled her. "What did you see?"

"There is an inch or two of broken board that is smooth. Only a saw could have made that cut. Worse, I think I saw some of the same marks on other boards across the middle of the bridge. Maybe, *maybe* we could explain away one board looking like that. Several?" He shook his head. "There's no other explanation."

She felt sick. "I meant what I said. I didn't want to be right about this."

"I know." Turning to look back at the bridge, he said, "I don't know what you want to do now. Do you want to go tell your parents?"

Susanna knew that was probably the right thing to do. But they hadn't even wanted her to take the shooting seriously. Finally, there was something about running home to tell her parents at her age. She wasn't a child, she was a grown woman who was fully capable of helping her family without asking for permission.

However, did she want to wander off to a sheriff's office with Neil Vance and not let anyone in her family know? Absolutely not. "I need to first go home and tell Amanda what I'm doing so she doesn't worry."

"And your parents?"

"If they are around, I'll let them know. But I'm going to tell them what I plan to do, not ask." She paused, watching his reaction. His eyes widened, but he didn't question her judgment.

Feeling a little more at ease, she continued. "After I do that, I'm going to go into town and see Deputy Beck."

"You're going to go right to the sheriff's office?" He frowned. "Deputy Beck is a good man, Susanna. I know him and I think he's fair and open-minded. But he might not believe you."

Just as he hadn't. Well, not at first. "I'm pretty sure Deputy Beck won't believe me at first. But I can't pretend it didn't happen."

"Of course you can't." Staring at the bridge again, he seemed to come to terms with something. "All right, then. We've got a plan. We'll go to . . . your house. There, you can tell them what you're doing, and then we'll go to see the sheriff."

"What? We? Neil, you don't have to do anything. Like I said, this ain't your problem."

"Of course I'm going to go with you. There's no way I would let you walk into the sheriff's office by yourself."

"Because you think I can't handle it?"

"Because I'm invested now," he said.

There was a new gleam in his eyes. Maybe it was respect? Maybe he was amused by her gumption? She had no idea.

As they stood there together in the morning cold, surrounded by a fresh blanket of new-fallen snow, Susanna reflected that she still didn't entirely trust Neil Vance, even though he'd helped her yesterday with her purchase and they'd gotten to know each other better when she'd dropped him home. And she still didn't completely understand him. She still felt that he had a lot of secrets that he was keeping from her.

There had even been a moment in the middle of the night, as she was tossing and turning, when she had wondered if he had been the person shooting at her buggy. After all, if there had been a hunter nearby, wouldn't he have come to her aid when he heard her crash?

Standing across from her with his thick arms folded over his chest, Neil watched her debate his help. Finally, he spoke. "I'm not about to stand back while you go talk to Deputy Beck on your own."

Suddenly, she realized that if he was going to accompany her to the sheriff's office, he was also going to be by her side when she went home to first talk to Amanda. "Are you going to be all right being at the house?"

"I think I need to be, don't you?"

"All right, then. Oh! Before we go, what should we do about the bridge? Do we need evidence or something? Do we take the piece of wood and show him, or ask him to come here with us?"

"I think . . . I think maybe we should take it with us. Just in case . . ." His voice drifted off.

Though he didn't finish his thought, he didn't need to. She knew what Neil was getting at. They needed to be prepared for any eventuality, even that someone might be upset that they were inspecting the bridge on their own. Or in case someone came by and decided to take the evidence before they could convince the deputy to accompany them back.

"I think that's a *gut* idea," she said.

She held her breath as he went back on the bridge, positioned himself awkwardly along the side, and then pulled up their evidence.

Then, without another word, she carefully crossed the creek where it was shallow, the rocks large, and the water frozen . . . and Neil walked by her side toward the house, which until very recently had always been called his.

NEIL WAS GLAD Susanna seemed to be lost in thought as they walked through the snowy field, slowly but steadily approaching his old house. The home he'd been born in and had always assumed he'd be spending the rest of his days in as well.

The house looked the same. White siding. Stone at the base of it, trailing up the side where the fireplace lay. The wide front porch with its dark-stained wood flooring. He'd stained it himself seven or eight months ago.

The closer they got, the slower Susanna seemed to be walking. The pensive expression on her face told him everything he needed to know. She wasn't looking forward to having him inside.

"I can wait out here, you know."

"Of course not."

"I don't want you to be uncomfortable."

She grinned suddenly as she pointed at the board under his arm. "I'm already uncomfortable. This is a pretty scary situation, Neil."

They were at the front door now. Carefully, he set the wood down, then waited for her to open the door.

When she did and he stepped across the threshold, he prepared himself to feel devastated. Hurt. Maybe even bitter and resentful.

But he didn't feel any of those things.

Maybe it was their furniture, or lack of it. They just didn't have much at all. While his family had had things on the walls and practically pouring out of cabinets and closets, now there was only empty space. It made the inside feel far bigger.

And quiet and peaceful. It also smelled like lemon oil. They'd been polishing baseboards and the woodwork.

In the main living room sat Susanna's sisters. Amanda was reading next to a smaller blond version of her. They both stared up at him in alarm before getting to their feet.

"What happened?" Amanda said as she strode forward.

Maybe her tone alerted them, but next thing he knew, out came both of their parents. Once again, looks of surprise gave way to wariness and alarm.

Obviously, they couldn't imagine another reason for him to be there unless something very bad had happened. That knowledge shamed him. His behavior over the last few weeks wasn't who he was. Once again, he vowed to do his best to make amends.

"I went over to look at the bridge this morning," Susanna said. "I saw Neil there."

When everyone's gaze turned to him, Neil said, "When

Susanna took me home yesterday, she mentioned her sister's accident on the bridge. Since I don't have to go into work until this afternoon, I went over to the Kaufmanns' to talk to Dale about it. When I saw Susanna's bright-blue scarf, I walked over to see what she was doing. The bridge can be really slick in the winter."

Susanna continued the story. "Neil didn't want me to climb up there, so he did."

"You believed me, Sue?" Traci asked as she joined them.

"I did. I'm glad I listened to you, too." She took a breath. "Everyone, Neil found something."

"What did you find?" Mr. Schwartz asked.

"I think someone cut the boards in the center of the bridge to make them weak."

Mrs. Schwartz shook her head. "Surely not."

"I wouldn't lie about something like that."

Susanna moved closer to his side. "We came back to tell you that we were going to go talk to Deputy Beck about it." Looking at her sister, she added, "I didn't want you all to worry about where I was."

"I'm glad you want to go, because I want to go, too."

"If you want to join us, you're gonna have to hurry to get ready," Susanna said.

"I can be ready in five minutes." Amanda trotted up the stairs.

Smiling shyly at Neil, Traci said, "Can I come, too?"

"Absolutely not," her father said. "And furthermore, I don't know how I feel about any of you going to the authorities."

Neil noticed that he treated his girls much different than his father had ever treated him. He wasn't forbidding them to do something.

"Daed, first I was shot at, and now someone tried to hurt us by sabotaging the bridge. I need to tell someone."

"But if that ain't the case . . ."

"Then it isn't," Neil said simply. "But I think we can all agree that we need to report this. To do nothing would be a mistake."

Mr. Schwartz studied him for a moment, then nodded. "I agree." Pointing to the stack of papers that was lining half of their kitchen table, he said, "I am knee-deep in bills, correspondence, and other paperwork with the house. Neil, thank you for helping us so much. We are in your debt."

Staring at Susanna's father, Neil was aware of two things. One was that the older man was trusting him. Even though he'd done little to deserve it, he was putting his daughters' care into his hands.

He was also realizing that he and his family had completely misjudged them. He and Roy and his parents had comforted their loss by painting a picture in their minds of the Schwartz family that was anything but true.

He wasn't sure why it had been so easy for them to do that. Maybe it had been easier to judge their faults instead of their own?

"It is I who is in your debt, Mr. Schwartz," he said. "I've been wearing my hurt about our family's problems on my sleeve. Because I've been so self-centered, I've been terribly rude to your daughter. I've already apologized to her, but I am hoping in time that you will be able to accept my apology as well."

"There is nothing to apologize for. You were hurting and were honest about it. I reckon you had some reasons, too."

"I think it would be best if we all moved forward," Mrs. Schwartz said. "After all, Christmas is just around the corner."

Susanna grinned at him. "My mother gets real excited about Christmas."

Her mother held up a hand. "Only a little bit."

When everyone chuckled again, he turned to Susanna. "Are you ready?"

"I will be as soon as Amanda gets here."

"I'm here," said Amanda.

Traci looked crestfallen. "I still think I should go, too. I could be a lot of help. I bet the sheriff would even want to hear about my accident."

"I bet he would, but he can come here to talk to you," Susanna said.

"But—"

"No more arguing, child," Mamm murmured. "You need to stay here and keep warm."

"Let's go," Susanna said. "The sooner we go, the sooner we'll get this over with."

Since Neil had just been thinking something along the same lines, he held open the door. "Ladies, after you."

CHAPTER 17

Tuesday, December 19

Though she tried not to be too obvious, Amanda kept a close eye on the way her sister and Neil Vance interacted. Susanna could sometimes be headstrong and impulsive. Those character traits had led her into trouble more than once. She sometimes charged ahead without weighing all the consequences, just as she tried to take on as much responsibility as she could so their mother wouldn't worry.

Back at the house, Amanda had been concerned that Susanna had been only pretending to get along with Neil.

But as she followed the couple back through the fields toward town, Amanda began to feel relieved. Their easy camaraderie showed that their relationship had evolved into something warmer. It was obvious that they'd come to some kind of understanding.

Amanda was glad of that. She and Susanna had enjoyed a large circle of friends back in Berlin. Though Susanna was assertive, she was also more socially awkward than herself.

She, on the other hand, excelled at making plans and enjoyed going to frolics and parties with lots of people, especially around Christmas and other holidays. The tension that had been brewing between Susanna and Neil had been weighing on her. She didn't want Susanna to put herself in a situation she wasn't sure how to handle.

As they got closer to the bridge, she noticed Dale standing next to it, obviously staring in confusion at the blank spot on the floor of the bridge.

"Looking for this?" Neil called out as they got closer.

"I was," Dale replied as he walked a little bit to the side, then scampered over the rocks and ice like a nimble deer. "'Course, I didn't expect to be seeing it under your arm."

"I'm ready to get rid of it myself," Neil replied with a grin.

Dale's eyes lit with amusement. "Hello, Susanna. Hi, Amanda."

Meeting his gaze, Amanda felt that familiar little pattering in her heart that she was beginning to realize only happened around him. "Hello, Dale."

After sharing a small smile with her, he turned back to his friend. "So, is there any specific reason you are now carrying part of the bridge with ya?"

"There is. We're about to go visit with the sheriff about it."

All traces of amusement faded from Dale's expression. "What's going on?"

"Our sister got hurt two nights ago when she was crossing the creek on the bridge." Pointing to the board, Susanna said, "I think someone deliberately sabotaged it."

There was no way Amanda was going to let her sister carry the weight of that claim by herself. "*Nee. We* think someone did. I agree with Sue completely."

Dale's eyebrows pulled together. "You certain about this, Neil?"

"As certain as I can be." Holding out the wood, he said, "Look at that cut there. Nature didn't make it."

Dale whistled under his breath. "Neil, you and me practically rebuilt that bridge about a year ago."

"I know."

"Now I've seen everything. I'm beginning to get pretty irritated. We just got that fencing repaired."

"After what happened with the fence and Susanna's buggy accident, we're pretty worried," Amanda said. She wasn't sure what Dale would think about her statement, but she wanted him to have no doubt about her feelings.

Dale shoved his hands into his pockets. "Since the bridge is half on our property, can I tag along?"

Neil looked a little unsure. "I don't know. Four seems like a lot of people to pop in on the sheriff."

"Dale and I can always stay off to the side or something," Amanda agreed.

Smiling at her, Dale said, "*Jah*. I can do that."

Neil narrowed his eyes at his friend. "We need to get going now, though. I've got to go to work this afternoon."

"Come on, then." He smiled and stepped to Amanda's side as both he and Amanda watched Neil help Susanna over the creek.

Susanna scrambled over it without seeming to even hesitate. Amanda was far more cautious, though.

Even as Susanna and Neil continued on, obviously thinking that they were right on their heels, she stared at the creek in building trepidation.

"You're going to think I'm silly, but I'm a bit afraid to cross it," Amanda admitted. When she was a little girl, she'd fallen into a creek one spring. The ice wasn't thick and her foot broke through. Next thing she knew, she was caught up in the current and was screaming for help.

Her father had pulled her right out. Actually, she probably wasn't in the creek more than two or three minutes at the most. But still, that memory clung to her like a sharp piece of glass. Deeply embedded and difficult to get out.

Looking at the frozen creek, she shivered a little bit. "I know I don't have anything to be afraid of. I know it's not deep." But the difference between the reality and the images her brain was inventing was staggering.

To her amazement, Dale didn't tease her. Instead he said, "I've got an idea. Let's cross this way. I'll go first, then you can follow."

Following did not sound easy! Glancing up, she noticed that Neil and her sister were watching impatiently from about twenty or thirty feet in the distance. "Actually, maybe I shouldn't—"

Before she could protest any more, he went out halfway and, balancing himself on two of the rocks, held out a hand. "Grab my hand and I'll help you."

"I'm afraid I'm going to yank you down or something."

"If you do, it doesn't matter. My feet will simply get wet."

Put that way, she nodded. Gingerly placing her hand in his, she stepped on the first rock. And . . . of course her boot slipped. "Oh!"

Dale slid his hand from her palm to her forearm, securing her better. "One step at a time. *Jah?*"

Releasing a ragged sigh, she nodded. *"Jah."*

Feeling like each foot was made of lead, she lifted her left foot and stepped onto the next rock. By the time she was halfway across, Dale had both feet on the opposite bank and was holding her opposite hand in his. Making her feel doubly secure.

She looked down. Was it her imagination, or was the creek running?

"Don't look down. Just look at me."

She could do that. Staring into his eyes, she stepped again. And again. Finally she had one, then both feet on solid ground.

She had done it! Feeling pleased, she smiled at Dale. "*Danke.* I'm so embarrassed that something so simple could have made my heart race like this. But thank you."

"No thanks are needed. I'm glad I was here to help."

She was, too.

"Dale? Amanda? Is everything all right?" Neil yelled.

"We're fine," Dale called out. "You go on ahead. We'll catch up in a minute."

Susanna and Neil turned around and started walking. They followed. After a moment, she and Dale seemed to both realize he was still gripping her elbow.

"*Sorry!*" Dale released her arm like it was on fire. "I think I was holding on to you so tight, you're going to have a bruise."

"I doubt that." She blew out some air. "I guess it's obvious that I fell in a creek years ago. I don't know why I'm not over it yet."

"Amanda, did you notice me complaining?"

Feeling herself blush, she shook her head. "I know you didn't."

"Then remember that, wouldja? I didn't mind helping

you. I won't mind helping you when we head back, either."
Winking, he said, "As a matter of fact, I enjoyed it."

"Oh?" She hoped she sounded composed, but she had a
feeling she sounded as giddy and awkward as she felt.

"Oh, to be sure. A man needs to feel like he's useful every
now and then, you know. It's good for one's ego."

She giggled before she could stop herself. Laughing while
they walked to the sheriff's office probably wasn't the best
way to behave.

But, she decided as she continued to walk by Dale's side
through the snowy pasture, maybe it wasn't the worst way to
act, either.

CHAPTER 18

Tuesday, December 19

The sheriff's office wasn't large. It was in an older-looking, single-story building made of limestone bricks. It was located next to a busy strip mall. There was a pharmacy, dry cleaners, convenience store, and haircut place.

Next to the modern signs, the sheriff's office looked stately. Susanna figured it might have been a house at one point. Inside, the first thing she noticed was a comfortable-looking gray-haired lady working at her computer at a small, serviceable desk. Beside her was a large glass of water, about a half-dozen file folders and spiral notebooks, and two cell phones. There was also a soup bowl filled with jelly beans.

When she, Neil, Amanda, and Dale walked in, the receptionist was on the office phone. She gave them a little smile as she gestured for them to be quiet.

Looking at each other, the four of them stood silently as a whole minute passed. Susanna looked around some more and noticed pretty garlands lining a couple of bookshelves on the other end of the room. A wreath made out of pine-cones and red ribbon hung over one of the doors.

After another minute, the receptionist finished her call, punched a couple of buttons on her computer, then carefully picked out two jelly beans from the bowl. Only after popping them into her mouth did she finally speak to them. "Now, how may I help y'all?" Her voice was surprisingly melodic, tinged with that husky Kentucky accent Susanna was beginning to be familiar with.

Susanna gulped when she realized that everyone was waiting for her to answer. It felt both empowering and a little scary. "We'd like to speak to Deputy Beck," she said at last, taking care to make sure her voice sounded firm.

Boy, was she glad that she wasn't there alone. Of course, if Neil hadn't been so pushy, worming his way into her business, she might have wandered around her property wondering what she should do.

She knew now that if she was standing here alone, she would have been shaking like a leaf.

The woman looked from her to Neil, who was standing about one foot behind her, holding the board. Then, popping another jelly bean into her mouth, she glanced at Amanda and Dale. "Deputy Beck is at lunch right now. He usually goes to see Lora over at Bill's Diner." Smiling slightly, she lowered her voice, like she was sharing something confidential. "Lora is his wife. They're newlyweds."

"I know Lora," Neil said. "When do you expect him back?"

The lady looked at the clock. "I'd say within the half hour, but it might be a little more." She shrugged. "Or a little less."

Behind her, Susanna could hear Amanda chuckle.

The receptionist pulled out a pad of paper. "You know what? I'm thinking it might be best if y'all went ahead and left a message. I can relay it the minute Deputy Beck returns."

But then what? It wasn't like the deputy could call any of them.

Making up her mind, Susanna said, "If you don't mind, we'd rather stay and wait for him. This is pretty important." She was also afraid if she left, she might not return until another incident happened to someone in their family. That wouldn't do.

The receptionist's expression turned wary. "Are you in trouble, hon?"

"*Nee.*" Then, she rethought that. If someone sabotaging her bridge wasn't trouble, then what was? "Well, maybe I am." Glancing behind her at Amanda, she said, "I mean, *we* are."

"I see." Eyeing the group of them with a far sharper expression, the lady murmured, "Any particular reason you brought in that piece of wood, Mr. . . . ?"

"Vance. I'm Neil Vance. And this is evidence."

She lumbered to her feet. "You know what? Let me see if Sheriff Brewer is available. Y'all have a seat now. Well, two of you can." She kind of aimlessly waved a hand at her bowl of jelly beans. "Help yourself, if you'd like."

As the receptionist disappeared down the hall, Susanna looked at the others. "Anybody want a jelly bean?"

Neil's lips twitched. *"Nee."*

"You would have thought she'd have gotten the sheriff right away," Amanda said.

"Maybe she's used to screening visitors," Dale surmised. "You girls take the chairs."

"Danke." Susanna smiled to herself as she sat down next to Amanda. In spite of the gravity of the situation, she couldn't help but feel comforted by the fact that the four of them were all getting along. Here they were, in a sheriff's office, no less, and the four of them were able to be amused by the brash receptionist.

As the minutes passed, Amanda leaned closer. "Are you starting to wish that we hadn't come here?"

"Nee. I'm glad we did. What's been happening is scary and needs to stop."

"I feel the same way. I'm glad I came along."

"Me, too."

"Are you nervous about speaking to the sheriff?"

Susanna shook her head. "I would probably be more comfortable with the deputy, but it isn't like I actually know him or anything." She turned to the men, who were leaning against the wall talking softly. "Any chance either of you already know the sheriff?"

Dale shook his head. *"Nee.* I've seen him around town, but I never had the occasion to speak to him."

"I've never met him, either, but that's likely a good thing," Neil said. "I only know Deputy Beck on account of Lora. She used to be Amish. Now she works at Bill's Diner."

"We should go over there one day, Sue," Amanda murmured. *"Jah."*

More minutes passed. The woman's computer beeped . . . or maybe she was hearing things and it was nerves; maybe she was uncomfortable with the silence. But she spoke again.

"I . . . well, I just want to say that I'm glad we're all together here," announced Susanna.

"Me, too," Neil said.

Amanda cleared her throat. "Does anyone have any idea who could have weakened the boards on purpose?"

"We probably don't need to talk about that now," Dale murmured.

"*Nee*, I think we probably should," Amanda countered. "After all, I know I didn't do it. No one in my family would have."

Dale frowned. "Well, I didn't do it, either. And my family uses that bridge a lot. We helped build it."

"What do you think, Neil?" Susanna said tentatively. "Can you think of anyone who would want us to get hurt?"

"Of course not." His voice was gruff.

She wondered if he was thinking that she suspected him. She hoped not. Because she didn't suspect him. But if it wasn't anyone in their three families, who would have done it?

It seemed like everyone else was thinking the same thing, too, because all four of them were staring into space when the receptionist at last reappeared, Sheriff Brewer by her side.

Sheriff Brewer looked to be in his early forties, had a cleanly shaven bald head and attractive gray eyes. He looked tall and strong. Capable of taking care of anything.

Susanna relaxed a little bit. If she was going to reach out to an outsider, she wanted it to be someone she could trust.

"Here they are, Sheriff," the receptionist said, slightly out of breath. "Right where I left them. Y'all help yourself to some jelly beans?"

"No, ma'am," Dale said. "But thank you."

"Anytime—" She cut herself off, obviously distracted. "You know what? I've already forgotten your names."

"I'm Neil Vance," Neil said, then gestured to the others.

"This is Susanna Schwartz. That's her sister Amanda, and this here is Dale Kaufmann."

"I'm Sheriff Pat Brewer."

The receptionist smiled, looking pleased. "Now that we know who everyone is, do you want me to take some notes or something?"

Sheriff Brewer looked slightly exasperated but resigned. "No. I'll take it from here, Hazel." Stepping forward, he held out a hand. "It's good to meet you all." After they shook hands, he pointed to the piece of wood that was now leaning against the wall. "I heard that y'all brought a piece of wood in here for us to talk about?"

"Yes. We'd like to tell you about what we found," Neil said.

"All of you?"

"Well, it was me and Neil," Susanna said.

"I came along to offer my sister support," Amanda said.

"And I came along because I helped build that bridge," Dale added. "And half of it is on our property."

"Our farms are next to each other," Amanda said. "Though, um, our farm used to be his," she added as she pointed to Neil.

"My office is kind of small." Looking at Neil, he said, "How about I speak with you and Susanna alone first? Then, if we need you, we'll come get you."

"That sounds fine," Amanda said.

Sheriff Brewer looked relieved. "Good. Susanna and Neil, y'all come on down to my office and fill me in."

Susanna looked warily at Amanda before following the sheriff and Neil. She really hoped he would have some answers for her. For them.

It turned out that there was a pretty good reason that Hazel was out of breath when she'd come back to them. The office was like a rabbit warren. "This building is a hundred years old," the sheriff said. "It was built when cave exploration was all the rage. I guess some of the early partners in the Horse Cave mine made a killing when they opened it up." As he turned right and then right again, he laughed. "The problem was that they built this place too well."

"How can that be a problem?" Neil asked.

"It's built too solid and looks too pretty to tear down, so people just kept adding onto it over the years."

"It's a lot bigger than I thought," Susanna said.

"It's a lot bigger than anyone ever believes it is," he said drily. Holding up a rubber band on his wrist, he grinned. "It's good for counting steps, though."

Neil chuckled. "One of my new bosses at Horse Cave Salvage tries to reach ten thousand a day."

"That's the goal." After they walked past a lunchroom, he spoke again. "Susanna, Hazel told me you came in looking for my deputy? Do you know Eddie?"

"Yes. I met him a couple of weeks ago. I had a buggy accident."

"It was just after Thanksgiving," Neil added.

"I remember that." He looked at her more closely. "So it was you?"

"*Jah.* Deputy Beck came to help me."

"I was there, too," Neil said. "I also know Deputy Beck slightly, because of his wife, Lora."

As they walked into the office, the sheriff whistled low. "That was quite a night. Eddie told me that his heart just about stopped when he saw you lying on the pavement. You're lucky to be alive."

Susanna nodded. "It was a scary night, for sure," she said as she looked around the spacious room. Right away, she noticed all the photos of the sheriff and his wife and family near his desk. There was also a rod and reel in a glass case hanging on the wall and a couple of plaques that looked like awards.

The furniture was dark wood and polished to a bright sheen. There were also two leather chairs with burgundy-colored seat cushions and a massive desk.

Folding his arms across his chest, he said, "Now. How can I help you both?"

Susanna looked at Neil pensively. Did he want to do the talking?

But he shook his head. "You go first. You're the reason we're here today, after all."

She was glad that he gave her that. It made her feel empowered and a little stronger. Releasing a breath, she said, "I should probably tell you about that buggy accident first. You see, I heard shots being fired. I had thought at first it was merely hunters . . . but the shots got closer. I felt pretty sure that someone was shooting *at* me."

Sheriff Brewer looked at her solemnly. "I see."

"Please don't tell me I was being foolish."

"I'm here to listen, Susanna. Now, did you tell Deputy Beck about your suspicions?"

"I didn't. At first, I was too hurt. Then, when I woke up, I thought it must have just been my imagination. But then some other things have happened."

He picked up a pencil. "Like what?"

"Well, next, part of the fence on our land was broken. Shattered into splinters. We don't have any cows or sheep or anything, but it was obvious someone did it just to cause damage."

"Did you have any idea about who might have done it?"

After looking warily at Neil, she nodded slowly. "Well, you see . . . at first we thought it might be Neil's family or our neighbors the Kaufmanns."

"Why?"

Just as she was about to attempt to explain, the sheriff's door opened and Deputy Beck entered. "Hi," he said with a polite smile. "Hazel told me y'all came looking for me?"

"Yes, but come in and join us."

"All right." As he sat down, he smiled at Neil. "Hey, I'm sorry I wasn't here when you arrived."

"It's all right. I heard you were over seeing Lora."

"Yeah." He shrugged. "I could give you some kind of excuse, but the truth is we're newlyweds."

"That's what your receptionist said."

"Hazel would. She's a talker." While they laughed, he stared at Susanna. "I know you, too."

"*Jah*. You helped me during my accident."

"Glad you're better," he said as he took a seat. "Sorry again for interrupting."

"Susanna here was just telling me about some damage that had been done to her property . . . and how her family had at one time suspected Neil's family of having something to do with it."

While the two officers stared at her and Neil Vance sat next to her stoically, Susanna was sure she had never been more mortified in her life.

Honestly, could she be handling this meeting any worse?

CHAPTER 19

Tuesday, December 19

Sitting in the reception area watching Hazel eat jelly beans and work on her computer was more painful than watching paint dry. Amanda was starting to feel fidgety. Beside her, Dale looked like he was feeling the same way. In the last two minutes, he'd shifted positions twice and was starting to look like he was regretting his offer to go with them.

She kind of was. She wanted to be there for her sister, of course. But waiting for Susanna to come out of a back room didn't seem all that supportive. She could have waited at home.

When the phone rang and the receptionist started asking the caller about all kinds of personal things, Amanda felt even more awkward. Overhearing someone's grievances with someone else's children made her feel like the worst sort of eavesdropper.

Unable to watch another jelly bean be consumed, Amanda leaned closer to Dale. "I know it's cold out, but would you like to go stand outside for a bit? I'm getting a little warm."

"I would. Standing outside sounds like a great idea." After informing Hazel of their plans, Dale held the door open for Amanda.

Luckily, the sun was out. Standing against the wall, which blocked the wind, made the area feel comfortable. Almost warm.

"This is a hundred percent better than watching Hazel work," Dale said.

Amanda had been kind of thinking that Hazel did a lot less working and a lot more chewing and talking than one might expect. Smiling at him, she said, "I couldn't agree more. Time never went so slow."

"How do you think their meeting is going?"

Amanda shrugged. "I hope okay. My sister isn't one to do things like this, so I imagine she's pretty nervous."

"Neil will look after her, if she needs looking after," he reassured her. "He doesn't get riled up about much."

"That's good. Susanna no doubt appreciates his support."

Dale stuffed his hands in his pockets. "Tell me about you. Are you going to get a job here? Or do you help out at home?"

"I used to babysit a lot in Berlin." Amanda felt her shoulders tense. She was proud of the work she'd done, but she knew some people didn't count babysitting as actual work.

"Really? Babies or little kids?"

"Any age. I like babies and children. It was fun. I knew a lot of people in the area, too, so I was plenty busy."

"You going to start doing that here?"

So glad that he really did seem interested in her work, she weighed her answer with care. "I thought I would, but now I don't know. I'll probably help out my parents as much as I can until things settle down."

"All these accidents have really shaken you up, haven't they?"

"*Jah*, it surely does have me rattled. Then, too, we live on a big farm now. It's a big house and a lot of land. Mamm and Daed might need my help."

"Will your father be hiring some men to help plow the fields?"

"I think so." Looking at Dale, she decided to share some more secrets. "We've never had a lot of money or a big farm before."

"But I heard that your father was a farmer. Was that not correct?"

"He is a farmer, but not on our land. He managed a big farm about an hour from us. He was gone most of the week, working for an Englisher while we lived in our duplex with Mamm back in Berlin."

"I'm surprised. I think Neil's family was under the impression that y'all were rich." He winced. "Sorry, I know I sound rude."

Maybe he was rude to be sharing that, but Amanda would take honesty over secrets any day. "I'd rather you knew the real me." Glancing at him, she said, "Are you disappointed?"

"About what? That your family ain't rich?"

"*Jah*. And the other things, too," she said hesitantly.

"Everything I'm discovering makes me happy that we met. I'm delighted that your father really does know how to farm and that you enjoy babysitting, too." The look he was sending her way was warm and kind. "No, I'm not disappointed in what I'm finding out at all."

"I'm glad."

"I'll talk to my father, but maybe he and I can lend your father a hand with the fields come spring."

"That's kind of you. But won't Neil be upset about that?" Of course, the moment she said it, Amanda wished she'd kept her mouth shut. Here, they were finally getting to know each other and she was bringing up something bad.

"You know? I don't think Neil would be upset anymore." Looking aggrieved, he said, "Now, his brother and father might be a different story."

"That's too bad."

"It is. And . . . I probably shouldn't have said anything about that." He shook his head. "This is awkward, isn't it?"

Amanda couldn't disagree. "I hope Susanna and Neil and the sheriff figure out what happened with that bridge—and who is going to so much trouble to make us feel so unwelcome. All I want to do is just get ready for Christmas."

"I couldn't agree more. This might be too bold, Amanda. But I am looking forward to seeing you under other circumstances."

"I feel the same way." Glancing at the entrance to the building, she said, "Let's hope and pray that they are making good progress in the sheriff's office."

"WE'LL DO OUR best, but I'm not sure I can make you any promises that we're going to be able to do much right now," Deputy Beck said as he led Susanna and Neil back through the maze of hallways to the reception area. "We'll ask around, but without any real concrete evidence, there's not a whole lot we can do at this time."

Susanna tried to wrap her mind around the fact that she'd taken such a chance by trusting the authorities and still nothing happened.

Neil simply nodded. "I appreciate your honesty, Eddie."

"You should remain vigilant, though. Keep a continued lookout. Watch for strangers or for anyone being where you don't think they should be. And if you happen to see something that points to any person in particular, let us know and we'll go from there," he said, his voice low and reassuring. Then, after glancing Susanna's way, obviously to make sure she realized he wasn't excluding her, he said, "If *you* encounter anything suspicious, anything at all, come back and talk to me."

Neil nodded, as if everything Deputy Beck was saying made perfect sense. "I'll do that."

The deputy paused. "Susanna, are you okay with this plan?"

She was disappointed, but it didn't seem like she had much of a choice in the matter. "I guess so."

"Feel free to come talk to me, even if Neil isn't with you. I'll tell Hazel to make sure she gets me right away if you come in."

"That is kind of you. Thank you."

Neil gave her a disbelieving look before they started walking again. She pretended she didn't notice that.

Because the truth was, she was pretty upset. It was her sister who had fallen through that bridge. Her sister who could have drowned. And that was only the bridge, never mind those gunshots and her buggy.

She was anxious about whatever was going to happen to them next. But the whole time she'd been sharing her suspicions, she'd felt as if the sheriff and Deputy Beck had only pretended to take her seriously. She'd felt like they were secretly thinking that she was exaggerating things. That she'd put two and two together and gotten sixteen.

They hadn't even been all that concerned about the cut

in the board. Even after Neil said that his family had helped build the bridge, they also pointed out that there was no way of knowing when it could have been made, and that someone could have been upset with someone in either Neil's *or* Dale's family years ago.

Or, it could have simply been a coincidence.

Now good manners meant that she was supposed to thank them for their time when actually they hadn't done much but waste hers. And though that sounded pretty harsh, that was how it felt.

When they arrived back at the reception area, Hazel was talking to a pair of police officers. "Men are here from Bowling Green, Deputy."

"Thanks, Hazel." Shifting, he looked at Susanna and Neil again. "We'll be in touch," he said, shaking both of their hands.

Practically before Susanna could say good-bye, he was talking to the other law enforcement men and walking down that long hallway again.

"Your friends went outside to wait for you," Hazel said.

"Thanks." Neil smiled gently down at her. "You ready, Susanna?"

Nodding, she let him get the door for her and followed him outside. How was she ever going to be able to tell her sisters that they were still essentially on their own—at least until something worse happened?

CHAPTER 20

I'm glad you had time to meet for lunch today," Dale said when he and Neil met outside Bill's Diner two days after their visit to the sheriff's office. "Yesterday, when I went for a walk with Amanda, she was still shaken up about our visit with Deputy Beck and Sheriff Brewer. Do you think Susanna feels better about everything?"

"I couldn't tell ya. I meant to stop by to see her yesterday evening, but I couldn't get away," Neil replied. "I do know that she was hoping that the sheriff was going to be shocked and upset about the bridge. I have to admit I felt the same way."

"I'm kind of surprised, too. Traci could have gotten really hurt."

"I'm trying to see things from the sheriff's point of view, but it's frustrating, you know?"

"*Jah.* I find myself worrying that the person who is bothering them might be someone we know. Then, just as suddenly, I realize that no one we know would deliberately set out to hurt them."

But someone was doing such things, Neil knew. Plus, hurting other people and their property didn't have to make sense to him. Thinking about the man who had been attacking women over in Munfordville recently, he said, "Some people are just twisted, though. There's no understanding the why of it."

Dale nodded. "Do you still want to go grab something to eat?"

"Sure." Since his choice was to either go home and face his father, who was still mourning their new situation, or enjoy a sandwich at Bill's before working an eight-hour shift, Neil knew there wasn't really much of a choice.

Soon after the hostess said hello, she placed them in Lora's section. The entire diner was decorated in lights. On the outside there were flashing colored lights. Inside silver garland lined the walls and some truly ugly-looking snowmen made out of socks dangled from the ceiling.

Dale frowned at the snowmen. "I don't reckon securing them by the neck was the way to go. It looks like they all got hanged."

He laughed. "It kind of does, at that."

They were still chuckling about it when Lora came to take their order. "What has the two of you in such a good mood?"

"Your hanging snowmen. They look a bit gruesome."

She wrinkled her nose. "I know. I tried to tell May to not hang them by the neck, but she wouldn't listen. I think they look more like Halloween decorations than Christmas." She shrugged. "What can I get y'all?"

After they ordered, Dale said, "Lora seems happy, doesn't she?"

"She really does."

"I was surprised when she came back to the area. But look what happened? She's now English, working at a diner, and married to a sheriff's deputy. She's happy, too."

"I'm glad for her," Neil said. "But is there a reason you're making a point to tell me all that? Or are you just stating your surprise?"

"I guess I was just thinking that Lora's life is a *gut* reminder to me about the Lord giving each of us choices in our lives."

Neil gritted his teeth. "Just say what you want to say."

"Only that a lot happened to Lora that could have made her bitter and discouraged. But instead of her acting that way, she seems to have learned from it all." Playing with the corner of the napkin in front of him, Dale mumbled, "At least it seems that way to me."

"Are you suggesting there's a lesson in there for me?"

"*Nee.*" Flushing a bit, Dale shrugged. "Well, maybe."

Neil's instant reaction was to tell Dale to mind his own business. He hadn't just given up his farm, he'd had to change his whole way of life. Instead of rising early with his brother and father to milk cows and tend to their other livestock, he was now working at Horse Cave Salvage.

Instead of tilling soil and planting crops on the same land that his grandfather had walked, he was working inside for a relative stranger.

Furthermore, he was trying to ease his family's financial burdens instead of simply assuming that his needs would be taken care of.

Neil's life was different in almost every way that counted. But maybe, he realized, Dale did have a point. Things were different, but he had adjusted. He'd also found happiness in his new job. And, well, if they hadn't had to move, then

Susanna wouldn't have come to Horse Cave. Already he was having trouble imagining life without her.

"You know better than most how hard these changes have been for me. But I'm getting better. So you may consider your point taken."

"Are you mad at me for trying to help you?"

"*Nee.* I know you mean well," he said as Lora returned with two hearty bowls of potato chowder and thick roast beef sandwiches.

After silently offering a quick prayer of thanks, they dug in. Neil figured it was his turn to do a little digging of his own. "It looks like you and Amanda are getting along all right."

"Anyone would get along with her. She's easy to talk to."

Intrigued, Neil smiled. "What have you been talking to her about?"

"Her, mostly. I realized that I knew who she was, but next to nothing about what she was like."

"Did you find out anything interesting?"

"I did." His smile grew. "She used to babysit for several families back in Berlin."

"And?" Dale had a huge family but no one in need of a babysitter. It was kind of strange that he cared about Amanda's babysitting jobs.

"Well, that means she likes *kinner.*"

"*Jah.* I guess she would, if she likes watching them. But what does that have to do with you?"

He averted his eyes. "Nothing."

No, it was something. "Wait a minute. Are you saying you're glad she likes *kinner* because you intend to have some with her?"

Dale sputtered on his sip of water. "Not tomorrow."

It was becoming hard not to start grinning. "But that's what you meant, right?"

Dale took another sip of water. "Well, yes." He held up his hand before Neil could even contemplate how to respond to that. "Now, don't you start acting like you are a font of wisdom about relationships and courting. All I'm saying is that I think that Amanda Schwartz, with her golden hair, blue eyes, sweet disposition, and her—"

"Experience with children?" he interjected.

"I was going to say her love of children means she's pretty special," Dale corrected with a grin. "I mean to get to know her better, too."

"I guess you do have a good point."

"I know I do." After taking another bite of his sandwich, Dale eyed Neil carefully. "Now, what about you and Susanna?"

"I ain't courting her. I'm trying to help her." And, he thought, to make amends for how rude I was when we met.

"That's it?"

"Ain't that enough?"

"Do you believe what she says about the gunshots and the board?"

"I thought I did, but after speaking to the sheriff and Eddie, I don't know. I guess it's safe to say that I believe she believes it."

Dale frowned. "I wouldn't tell her that."

"I haven't. What did your father say about the broken fence?"

"That Mr. Schwartz was right on the money. Someone deliberately broke it."

As Neil finished his sandwich, he contemplated what he

should do next with Susanna. Leave her alone? Talk to his parents and tell them that he'd met the Schwartz family and believed they'd gotten them all wrong?

Looking at the clock above the door, he pushed his plate away. He needed to get to work. He spied Lora standing by the kitchen door. She was talking on her cell phone. When she noticed him staring, she hung up and hurried over.

"We need our check, Lora. I've got to get to work."

"Um, okay." As she flipped through her pad of paper, she said, "Listen, that was Eddie. He called to tell me that he was going to be working late."

Obviously alerted by her tone, Dale said, "Everything okay?"

"I don't know. Dispatch just took a call. There's a fire on your old property, Neil."

"You sure?"

"Oh, yeah. The fire truck is on the way there now."

"So are *we*," Dale said as he tossed a twenty on the table.

Neil was right behind him. "Lora, I hate to ask you, but could you call the salvage for me and explain that I'll be late?"

"Sure. But do you really think you should go over there? Not to be mean, but their fire ain't your problem anymore."

"I don't have a choice," he said as he strode out of the diner.

Right then and there, it didn't matter where the fire was. All he cared about was that Susanna might need him.

CHAPTER 21

Thursday, December 21

The first thing Susanna noticed were flashing lights. Then she noticed the trace of smoke in the air. There had been a fire. Though her brain was urging her to run, she froze. "Amanda, that's our house, ain't it?"

Her sister looked just as taken aback. She inhaled sharply before racing forward without saying a word.

Susanna started running, too. As she got closer, she spied the remains of a shed near two men with fire hoses. She stopped abruptly. A thousand questions ran through her head, but there was only one that mattered. "Is my family all right?" she asked the first person she found.

The fireman blinked at her in surprise before bending down so they were eye level. "They're fine," he answered immediately. While she processed that and tried to get a grip on herself, he continued in a calm, steady tone. "Only an old wooden shed burned down, miss. That one there on the edge of your property. No one was nearby. Not even any animals."

"You're sure?" Her voice was trembling, but she didn't care.

"I'm positive, miss. Believe me, I would never sugarcoat something like that."

Susanna liked how he phrased that. His words sounded strong and sure. The way his voice sounded thick and almost blanketed in his Kentucky drawl convinced her that he was speaking straight from the heart.

Feeling a bit better, she began scanning the area for her family. There were several firemen and law enforcement people there . . . she was able to pick out her father. But where was everyone else?

Just as she started to panic, her mother rushed toward her.

"Susanna! Praise God!"

Susanna noticed that Mamm was wearing a light-gray dress, black stockings, and boots; her blond hair was neatly pinned up under her white *kapp*, but she didn't have a scarf or a black bonnet on for warmth. She didn't even have on a sweater.

"Sue, thank the good Lord that you and Amanda are finally here where I can see you," Mamm said as soon as they reached each other. Enfolding her in her arms, she said, "I knew you were in town, but this has surely got me rattled."

Susanna hugged her tightly, all while attempting to ascertain just how chilled she was. "I couldn't believe it when I saw all the emergency vehicles. I was so scared, at first I could hardly move."

"Daed was inside the kitchen with me, having some soup, when we heard a loud bang," Mamm said as she pulled away. "I didn't know what was happening."

"Are you all right? Is Daed?"

"We're fine. Just shaken up, but that will pass, with the Lord's help."

"We need to get you warm, Mamm. Don't you want to go inside?"

"I can't. I need to see what is happening."

Susanna supposed she couldn't argue with that. She could no more go sit inside than walk back toward town. After hastily unbuttoning her coat, she held it out to her mother. "Here, now. Put this on." When Mamm tried to refuse, Susanna started wrapping it around her mother's frail shoulders herself. "Please, Mamm. You were so sick."

Without another word, her mother fastened the black wool cloak around her shoulders. Then, as if she couldn't bear to stop touching her, she grasped Susanna's hand again. "Though I knew you and Amanda were in town, I am still mighty relieved to see that you are standing here safe and sound."

"I feel the same way." Remembering Amanda's actions, she grinned. "When I saw the fire truck, I froze. But our Amanda just started running over here, just like she was a track star."

Chuckling softly, Mamm pointed to her left. "Looks like your sister got here just fine on her own. She's over there talking to your father and the deputy."

When Susanna turned, she noticed that Dale and Neil were standing off to the side, speaking with another fireman. It seemed like just about everyone she knew had arrived . . . but she didn't see her younger sister.

"Where's Traci?"

A new line of worry entered her mother's expression. "Traci? Well, your sister was kind of shaken up, and no wonder, too. She wanted to go sit with Midge."

"But she's all right?"

"*Jah*. She is fine." A light of humor lit her mother's blue eyes. "She simply needed to be with our new horse. She does love those animals."

"Indeed. She always has." At last Susanna felt like she could draw a real breath. Midge, their new buggy horse . . . they'd all felt the loss of Star deeply. God had given them a blessing when Daed found Midge, an eight-year-old mare with an easygoing disposition and, they were discovering, a fondness for carrots.

She'd been an older couple's horse, and hadn't gotten much attention or exercise the last couple of years. She seemed delighted to be a part of their family, and especially loved Traci.

"Do you want me to go check on her, Mamm?"

"You can if you'd like, but I don't think there is any need. I imagine Traci is likely pleased to be away from all of the commotion around here." Looking around at the trucks parked in the field, especially the one that still had its blinking lights on, Susanna's mother wrapped her arms around her waist. "I'm grateful for these men, of course. They got here in time to prevent that fire from spreading. But it is quite jarring at the moment."

"Everything is going to be okay, Mamm."

Tears filled her mother's eyes. "I hope so, but I fear that we might have said that one too many times. I feel as if I'm in an awful dream. Before we moved here, I had never spoken to a policeman. Now I know their names." Swiping her eye with the side of her hand, she shook her head. "It's a lot to take in."

Susanna couldn't disagree. "I feel the same way."

"It's becoming obvious that someone doesn't want us here."

She was so worried about her mother's health and state of mind, Susanna pushed aside her desire to stand in the thick of things. "Mamm, how about we go inside and I make you some tea? Daed and Amanda can tell us what the police and firemen said later on."

She shook her head. "I'm not sick." Giving Susanna an exasperated look, she added, "You don't need to worry about me any longer. Stop fussing. I am fine."

Stung, Susanna tried to hide her hurt. "You know I fuss because I care."

"And I appreciate that. But I am fine." With a new edge of steel in her voice, Mamm said, "I'm not going to start hiding, either. I want to know all that is being discussed . . . and what I can do to stop all this nonsense." Before she could comment on that, Mamm breathed a sigh of relief. "Oh, good. It looks like your father knows something. I'm going to go see what it is."

Susanna was about to follow but stopped when she watched her mother reach for her father's hand. They didn't often do things like that, so she decided to give them some time alone. Instead, she gave in to temptation and walked over to where Dale and Neil were standing with Deputy Beck.

The three men stopped their discussion when she approached.

"Hey, Sue," Neil said the moment she got close. "You okay?"

"I don't know. I still am not sure what happened."

"As far as we can tell, someone set fire to your shed," Deputy Beck said. "Your father said he heard a sudden loud noise and then the fire erupted."

The way they were looking at each other, like that was significant, was confusing. "What does that mean?"

"That the fire wasn't an accident," Neil said.

Not an accident. It had been set on purpose. "You sound so sure," she whispered.

"Of course, everyone is going to be investigating it further and will be looking for accelerants or any other clues that it was set deliberately, but it seems likely. I'm sorry, Miss Schwartz," the deputy said.

Staring at the smoking embers, she murmured, "Is there a way to figure out who set it?"

"The fire marshal will have a better answer, but it's going to be tough," the deputy said after a moment. "Short of trying to trace whoever purchased the accelerant or starter? I don't know what they can do."

She looked at her parents, who were standing close together, her mother clinging to her father's hand for support. "My mother is crying, Deputy Beck. And my parents—all of us—have been through so much already. When are you going to start taking everything that is happening to us seriously?"

Neil frowned. "Susanna, I know you're upset, but we already talked about this. You mustn't blame—"

"No, I can take it," Deputy Beck said. "She's exactly right. I fear we should have been working more proactively on this case."

That sounded a lot like he knew they hadn't done much but were now going to start trying harder.

That was small comfort. Too many awful things had happened already.

First, she'd been in the buggy accident. She'd not only gotten a concussion, but she'd been banged up and bruised. Then the bridge Traci had been walking on broke. She'd fallen into the frozen creek and got her dress stuck. Traci could have drowned!

And now, with the shed set on fire—any one of these things could have seriously hurt or killed members of her family!

Feeling tears well in her eyes, she first tried to blink them away, then swiped at them angrily with her hand. But they still kept coming.

Almost at once, three handkerchiefs were pressed into her hands. Grabbing one, she turned and started walking. Crying was not going to help anything. She needed to get control of herself!

But unfortunately, her body didn't seem in any hurry to listen to what her head was saying. Instead of dissipating, her tears increased. Soon they were wracking her body. Leaning against a wooden post, she sighed and gave in. Maybe what she needed to do was simply cry. Cry hard and let out everything she was feeling.

Then, suddenly, she wasn't alone any longer.

"Hey," Neil said as he wrapped his arms around her. "I'm sorry."

Giving in to temptation, she rested her head against his chest. Around a hiccup, she said, "What are you sorry for?"

"For trying to make you stop," he said, pulling her even closer. "You have every reason to be upset. Every reason and every right. Cry all you want."

Part of her wanted to snap at him. To tell him that she didn't need his permission. But again, it seemed she was defenseless against a higher power. The tears started again.

"I'm going to get you all wet," she mumbled.

"I don't care." He rubbed her back. "I've got nothing else planned for the day and plenty of shirts to change into."

"I . . . I hope I don't soak multiple shirts."

"Shh, now. Just relax."

His arms were warm. His body, so much bigger than hers, was solid and so strong. But what drew her to him, she knew, was his kindness.

Finally, she closed her eyes and sighed deeply. He was right. She needed to try to relax. She needed to give herself permission to fall apart. She now had someone to help pick up the pieces.

And if someone was now setting outbuildings on fire, things had escalated, indeed.

CHAPTER 22

Thursday, December 21

I didn't realize Dale Kaufmann and Amanda Schwartz had gotten so close," Deputy Eddie Beck said about a half hour later.

After Neil had enfolded Susanna in his arms and let her cry, she'd gone back to check on her mother and father. Neil had intended to return to Dale, but he saw that he was speaking quietly with Amanda. Minutes later, Dale wrapped his arms around her and was whispering in her ear.

And Amanda? Well, she looked like only Dale could ease her worries.

Looking over at the couple, Neil murmured, "I didn't realize it, either. I mean, I knew there was something between them . . . but not that."

Inwardly, he was wincing. Did he sound as tongue-tied as he felt? He was happy for Dale, he really was. But there was also a little bit of jealousy going on, he realized.

He was jealous of how easy and smooth Dale and Amanda's relationship was progressing. It was so different than he and Susanna. Though they were growing closer, the farm and their uneasy first conversations felt like obstacles they needed to overcome.

Eddie was boldly gazing at the couple and shrugged. "Maybe it's a sudden thing. That happens, you know."

"I heard it does," Neil teased. Actually, he figured just about everyone in Hart County knew at least some of how Eddie Beck and his new bride, Lora, got together. It all started when Eddie had moved to the area and started eating at Bill's Diner. Lora worked there but hardly ever waited on him. He'd watched her from a distance for weeks.

Then, just a few months ago, he'd been called to Lora's house for a disturbance. He interviewed her. Something must have happened during their conversation because then Lora started waiting on him at the restaurant.

During this time, a man had been attacking women in Munfordville. Lora had been one of those women. Rumor had it that Eddie had sat by her side for hours while she recuperated in the hospital.

Later, she'd been coherent enough to identify her attacker, so she had helped solve the case.

And Eddie? Well, he'd been so smitten, he'd wasted no time in making her his wife.

Their roller-coaster love story did nothing to ease the tension inside of Neil. He was afraid for Susanna and her family. Whoever was targeting them was getting bolder and bolder. "What is going to happen now? This all needs to stop."

Looking back at Neil, the deputy's gaze was intent. "I completely agree. I'll be conferring with Sheriff Brewer, but I would guess we'll be paying a call on the Schwartzes to see if they have any idea of why someone might want to target them."

"Let me know if I can help."

Eddie raised his eyebrows. "Susanna mentioned that they'd felt like a lot of people were mad at them for moving here and buying the property. Do you think there is any truth to that statement?"

Knowing how angry he and his parents had been, Neil couldn't help but nod. "I'm afraid so." Because no doubt everyone already knew this, he said, "My family was pretty upset about the transaction. That's no secret."

"Maybe we should talk about that. You resented them for buying your farm?"

"I did." Wearily, he continued. "And you don't have to tell me that we had it for sale. I think we all had a lot of hurt feelings. The sale felt rushed. We had hoped for more money for the property."

"Do you think anyone in your family was so mad that they sought vengeance?"

"And started breaking bridges and setting fire to sheds? *Nee.*"

"But you agree that there might be someone in your family who feels that you had every right to wreak havoc on the Schwartz family."

"Perhaps." He was thinking of Roy, who acted so easygoing and happy to be working for the Costa family . . . but he was good at hiding his feelings; and his father, whose fault it was that they were in this situation in the first place, and who so resented that he was now at his younger brother's beck and call.

Then there was his Uncle Joseph. He had given thousands of dollars to Neil's father with the expectation that the farm would be given to him so it would remain in the family. But instead of doing that, Neil's father had insisted on selling the farm to strangers.

Uncle Joseph had to feel betrayed and used. But would he take it out on the Schwartz family?

Finally, Neil knew that even he and his mother had entertained some dark moments. More than once Neil had fallen asleep wishing that the Schwartzes would feel some kind of pain for how they handled the sale.

When the deputy continued to say nothing, only watched him intently, Neil was uncomfortably aware that he'd indicated that every member of his family was a prime suspect.

"Hey, now, just because we were upset, that doesn't mean that we did anything," he blurted. "It's a long way between missing one's farm and setting fire to it."

"Of course. I didn't say I thought you did anything."

"My family doesn't have anything to do with this." At least, he hoped and prayed that was the case.

Deputy Beck adjusted his jacket. "All right, then." He kind of huffed as he pulled out his smartphone. "I'd best get on my way. Brewer doesn't pay me to stand around and chat, you know. It's been good to talk to you. I'm sure we'll chat again real soon." He smiled, but the warmth didn't reach his eyes.

"*Jah.* Sure," Neil said awkwardly.

Watching him walk away, Neil realized that Eddie hadn't actually accused him of anything. But he hadn't said that he didn't suspect him, either. And what did that mean, when he said that they'd be talking soon? Was that a hint?

He hoped not. When he got home, he was going to have to have a real close conversation with his parents and Roy. Actually, they should probably get together and do some thinking about who could be a suspect besides them. Maybe he should talk to Junior at work about that, too. Junior was a good manager and seemed to trust him.

Yeah. They definitely needed to do some thinking about who didn't seem happy that the Schwartz family had moved to town . . .

As he stood on the land that he always thought he'd inherit, Neil realized that something had just happened. This place didn't feel like home anymore.

Instead, when he thought of home, he thought of that cramped house that they'd all imagined was too small but seemed to still hold everything that they really needed. Home was where his family was. It was where the people he cared about were.

And when he thought of his job, he didn't think about this farm, he thought about his many responsibilities at Horse Cave Salvage. His perception had changed before he was even aware of it. Maybe before he was even ready for it.

But still, it had happened.

Why was that?

CHAPTER 23

Thursday, December 21

When Deputy Beck joined Sheriff Brewer and her father, Susanna noticed her mother was returning to the house and the fire truck had left. She knew where Traci was now—but Amanda . . . ?

Well, she'd finally left the comfort of Dale Kaufmann's arms but was still talking very closely to him. Her face was tilted up and she was smiling into his eyes like he was wonderful.

She'd never seen her sister look at a man like that before. It took her off guard, but Susanna couldn't say that she found fault with Amanda's choice. So far, Dale Kaufmann had been very nice and solid. He also had a kind way about him.

But still, she couldn't understand when their attraction had blossomed into something so easy and almost peaceful. What had they discovered about each other so fast? Several times when she and Neil had made any sort of connection, it seemed to be accompanied by another three steps back.

She had, though, just moments ago found solace in his arms. But after he released her, she'd been so flustered that she'd run off to check on her parents. Now, she realized, she still felt unsure how to act around him.

Butterflies filled her insides as she saw she was about to find out. Neil was walking toward her, looking so solid and strong . . . and clearly worried.

"Ach, Susanna," he said, his voice as deep and scratchy with emotion as it had been the night they'd first met. "I'm *so* sorry about all this."

"There's no need for you to apologize. None of this is your fault."

His expression turned pained. "I know that, but I still feel like I'm a reminder of everything that your family has been going through since you moved to Horse Cave. You've had such high hopes, but all that's happened since you've gotten here is one tragedy after another. I can't think of a single thing that would give you any comfort."

Susanna was struck by both his honesty and his compassion for her perspective. He'd described what they'd been going through fairly well, too. But not in its entirety. "You are comforting me just by being here."

"Yeah, right." His lips pursed. "I'm sorry. I'm not trying to make this about me or my feelings. I am only trying to be honest with you. As honest with you as I possibly can."

If he could be completely frank, then she could, too. "I appreciate that. And you are exactly right. Our life has felt as topsy-turvy as some of these windy, hilly roads around here." Looking out toward the road, she said, "Some days I feel like all I can do is simply hold on or I'm going to fall."

"And if you fall?"

Well, that was the crux of it, wasn't it? She feared either her heart or her body was going to be hurt.

Unused to voicing her fears, she looked at him hesitantly. "If I fall, Neil, I know I won't break . . . but I don't know how easy it will be to get back on my feet."

"If you fall, I hope you will reach out a hand. If you do, I have a feeling you might be surprised about who is going to help you get back up."

"Are you talking about yourself or the Lord?"

A glimpse of humor appeared in his eyes. "Maybe both?"

She chuckled. "If both of you are here for me, I will be mighty grateful."

He shook his head in wonder. "I never imagined you'd be talking to me like this." His throat worked as he visibly struggled for words. "I'm glad of it."

"Neil, I promise, I never thought you did this."

"I never would deliberately set a fire like that. Never."

"I believe you. But why . . ." She broke off, unsure of how to verbalize her question. Finally, she just asked the obvious. "What is wrong?"

"I am afraid the sheriff suspects someone in my family has something to do with all of this."

A chill raced through her. "Did he say that?"

"Not in so many words, but it was implied. We talked about who has the most to gain from running you off the farm. Deputy Beck pointed out that my family does."

"Are you confessing that you've been behind all of this?" She was teasing.

"*Nee!* Of course not."

"Then why are you so worried?"

"Because I can see how the sheriff might think that way. I'm embarrassed to say that no one in my family kept their pain at bay. We all shared our frustration openly. It was wrong."

He looked so upset, she yearned to comfort him. But how could she? He was right—his family's resentment was so strong that it had made their first weeks here both awkward and painful. "Do you still blame my parents for buying your farm?"

"*Nee*. You did what anyone would have done. You found a good deal and took advantage of it. Why wouldn't you want to do that?" He exhaled. "We, well, Roy and I, we now realize that we put the blame on your *daed*'s shoulders because coming to terms with the fact that it was our father who lost our savings was too hard."

"Is that what happened?"

"*Jah*. He borrowed money he couldn't repay, and he eventually made the choice to sell the property instead of just giving it to my uncle."

This was the first time she'd heard him mention an uncle. "Who is he?"

"My uncle Joseph." Grimacing, he said, "He's my father's younger brother."

"You don't look like you care for him that much."

He laughed. The sound was the opposite of joyful. Instead, it was hard and bitter. "I do and yet I don't." Looking bleak, he said, "I guess my feelings for him could be best described as complicated."

"Ah."

He blinked, as if something had just occurred to him. "Listen, Susanna, you need to know something. It's something I'm going to have to talk to Sheriff Brewer and Deputy Beck about, too. Even if y'all hadn't bought our farm, we still would have had it up for sale. We couldn't afford the land and my father would never give in to my uncle." After a pause, he added, "And even if y'all left tonight, we wouldn't move back."

"Because you can't afford it."

"Because we can't afford it . . . and because we've moved on. All of us have realized that this land was like an albatross around our necks for years. Now that the weight of the bills and debts isn't weighing us down, we're beginning to find happiness in other places."

"Really?"

"I enjoy my job at Horse Cave. And Roy, well, I think he has enjoyed working at the Englisher's farm. It's a big place, really big, actually. The family who owns it seems to value him, too."

"That's important."

"I've told him much the same thing." His eyes brightened. "Even my mother has found new life, baking for others. She's got quite a business started, selling to some area gift stores and bed-and-breakfasts. Why, you should see how busy she is right now."

"If she needs help, let me know. I like to bake, too. I mean, if she wants to know me."

Neil looked relieved to not be talking about his family's pain. "I know she'd love your help. And I know she is going to want to know you, Susanna."

"Because of all of this and our connection?"

"Probably. But also because of the way I can't seem to stop talking about you."

Once again, that warm rush of happiness filled her, taking her by surprise. "You've been talking about me with your family?"

"*Jah*. I can't seem to stop." His gaze swept across her face, obviously trying to take in every nuance that he could glean. "Am I the only one who has been feeling this connection?"

She shook her head slowly.

He released a sigh. "What do you think about coming over one day soon? You can meet everyone."

"They wouldn't get mad that I was there?"

"They would be pleased. And once you start talking about cookies and cakes, my mother is going to glow, she's going to be so excited."

"Hardly that."

"You might be surprised, Susanna. Don't forget, she lives in a house filled with men." When she smiled at that, he said, "So, will you?"

She nodded. "I will. I think I would like to come over to your house very much."

CHAPTER 24

Friday, December 22

The first thing Neil noticed when he woke up was that the coffee had been made and his father was pacing on the packed dirt in front of the house. Neil didn't have to wonder what had his father so agitated. No doubt he was still thinking about yesterday's fire. Neil knew he was.

Even if the property wasn't theirs anymore, knowing that someone had wanted to destroy part of it felt extremely personal. His grandfather had built that shed. His father had asked him and Roy to fix some of its warped boards when they were nine and ten. It had been their first "real" job he'd given them to do on their own. And now it was gone. He felt as if someone had deliberately meant to taint the legacy they'd left behind.

Though Neil had relayed everything he knew to Roy and his parents the minute he'd gotten home, each bit of information had only seemed to prompt another round of questions or worries.

His mother had even teared up. She'd wondered if somehow their family was at fault, since none of them had been shy about how hard it had been to leave their home.

Neil had spent a restless night tossing and turning on his pallet on the floor. His dreams had been filled with Susanna's green eyes, Deputy Beck's questions, and Uncle Joseph's words about how his father hadn't wanted him and Roy to sleep in the big house.

He didn't know if any of it meant anything. But it sure felt as if the Lord was trying to tell his unconscious something important.

After filling up his own mug with hot coffee, he shrugged on his favorite sweatshirt and knit cap, then went out to join his father. As he expected, the December air was damp and frigid. Neil reckoned it would do more to wake him up than the hot coffee ever could.

Daed glanced over in surprise when Neil walked out the door. After hesitating for a brief moment, he seemed to gather his thoughts. "Morning, son," he said quietly as he walked toward Neil. "I didn't expect to see you up for another couple of hours. We were up late last night."

"We were, but it looks like you've been up for quite some time."

"I have. I guess I can't stop thinking about that fire on our old property. It's such a shock, you know?"

"*Jah.*"

"I realized this morning that I had forgotten to ask you about something else."

"What was that?"

"Before you came home, did you stop by Joseph's house and speak to him about the fire?"

"*Nee.*" An uneasy feeling that he couldn't explain settled

in his chest. "Did you want me to? If so, I can go over there now."

"No! I mean, there ain't no need for that. He probably wouldn't even remember what shed you were talking about."

"Are you sure? You told me once that you and he used to play hide-and-seek near there."

"You got that wrong, Neil. Joseph and I didn't ever play there."

His father was staring at him directly, practically willing him to take back his words. Neil knew he wasn't wrong, though. He and Roy had played near that shed, too. They'd often joked with each other, saying that they hoped their relationship wouldn't fall apart like their father and uncle's had.

He let it go, though. After all, did it even matter? The shed was gone now. "It's a blessing the Schwartz family didn't have anything of worth inside there."

"A true blessing, indeed." His father sighed. "I know there ain't anything we can do to help them, but I feel like we should go over there and lend our support."

That took Neil by surprise. "What do you mean?"

He shrugged. "I don't know," he mumbled. "Maybe offer to lend a hand?"

Neil had a feeling that the Kaufmanns were already going over there today to help clean up the remains of the fire. By the time Neil and his father could get there, most likely everything would already be done. "I guess I could ask," he murmured.

"I'm sure there's no need to ask permission to go over there. After all, all we want to do is help clear the land." Looking more assured, he added, "Then, of course, we need to discover what they know."

"About what?" asked Neil.

"About who they think set the fire."

"I believe they are letting Sheriff Brewer figure that out."

"Maybe so, though they must have some ideas. You know, they've experienced so many accidents and scares. I don't know how they are sleeping each night. Actually, I'm mighty surprised they haven't packed up and left yet."

His father really did sound surprised. Realizing his hand was unsteady, Neil clenched it into a fist. "Susanna seems to think that's what the perpetrator's goal has been. For whatever reason, he wants them to pack up and move back to Ohio."

"But they haven't." He smiled grimly.

That response made him feel uneasy. Pushing it away, Neil said, "I'm really worried about Susanna. Yesterday's fire really scared her."

"I bet." Daed lifted the mug to his lips, seemed to notice that it was empty, then set it back down again. "I feel somehow responsible for their troubles, Neil."

"Why do you say that?"

"You know how I acted." He waved a hand. "How I've been acting. I knew I failed you all when I lost so much money." His voice turned hoarse. "First, I believed that man who said investing in the area south of here was a good idea. I didn't even check to see if it was habitable. So stupid."

"Daed, it was an honest mistake. You weren't the only man in Hart County to be taken in by his smooth words."

"You're right. I wasn't. But I was one of the few who was too proud to confess my mistake to my wife and sons. Instead, I only confessed to Joseph."

"And he took advantage of you."

His gaze sharpened before his expression went flat again. "Did he? I don't know anymore. All I do know is that the more I owed, the more reckless I became. Gambling is a sin, yet I did it anyway."

Neil didn't want to rehash all of his father's mistakes. It didn't matter, what was done was done. But he did want to know more about Joseph. "I talked to Uncle Joseph the other evening."

"Why?"

The question caught him off guard. "He was sitting alone when I was walking home. I felt sorry for him, I guess. I ended up sharing a cup of coffee with him." Before his father could say anything about that, he continued. "He said that he offered to have Roy and me live with him."

"He told you that?" Pure bitterness filled his voice. Again, Neil was caught off guard.

"You never mentioned that to me. Did you tell Roy?"

"Of course not." His father was staring at him with an expression full of scorn. "You don't belong over there. Not with him."

Now Neil felt even more confused. Switching tactics, he said, "Daed, if you want to go see the Schwartzes, I'll go with you. Mamm, too."

"You don't think they'd mind?"

"From what Susanna has told me, I think they'd be happy that you're reaching out to them. Actually, I asked Susanna to come over one day and spend some time with Mamm. Susanna likes to bake cookies, too."

The wrinkle in his brow eased. "That would make your mother happy. I'll go talk to her about that, and about visiting the old place. Maybe she'll want to go visiting as well."

Neil was pretty sure that his mother wasn't the one who needed encouragement to go to their old property. "Let me know what you want to do. I plan to see Susanna regardless."

"The two of you really have gotten close, haven't you?"

"We have. Susanna is bold and kindhearted, and tries so hard to make everyone around her feel better. I really admire her."

"She sounds a lot like someone else I know," Daed said with a slight smile.

"*Danke.*"

He sighed. "The sun is still rising, which means it's time I had my breakfast and another cup of coffee. Then I had better go see what your uncle has in store for me."

There it was again, the steady reminder that something wasn't right between the two of them. "Maybe you should look for something different to do."

His father raised his eyebrows. "Different than what?"

"Different than farming. Different than working for Onkle Joseph."

"I canna really do that, Neil. Farming is all I know. It's all I'm good at."

"But what about working for someone else? The Costas treat Roy really well."

"I don't know, Neil. Plus, I owe Joseph so much."

"You paid him back, Daed. You don't owe Uncle Joseph anything anymore."

"I'd like to say I only owe him money, son, but that wouldn't be true. And he? Well, he owes me something, too."

While Neil stood there, trying without success to make sense of his words, his father walked back into the house, his coffee cup already forgotten.

Neil reached for it, intending to give it to his father, then decided to take care of it himself. As he walked back to the house, Neil realized the errand had much in common with how his relationship with his father had become. No longer was Neil depending on him for either support or comfort. No, more often than not, he was the one who was looking out for his father.

He just hoped he was doing enough for his father. If he wasn't, Neil wasn't sure what would happen to him next.

WHEN NEIL ARRIVED at Horse Cave Salvage two hours later, he had a good sweat even though it was below the freezing mark outside. His spirit had been so disturbed, he'd race-walked practically the whole way to work.

Unfortunately, all that had happened was he had arrived sweaty and tired for an eight-hour shift. He ran into the washroom to clean up.

When he saw his glassy eyes and flushed cheeks in the mirror there, he wished he would have taken some time to rest and pray before walking into the employees' entrance. He looked as stressed and distraught as he felt.

Since it was too late to do that, he walked over to Diane. She was the store manager, and his boss when Junior, the owner, wasn't around. "Okay if I get to work early today?"

Diane's gaze softened on him like it always did. "You know we are never going to fault you for wanting to work, Neil."

"You sure Junior won't mind about the overtime?"

"He'll be fine with you working an extra hour. We just got in a pallet of bulk foods." Her lips curved up. "We need every strong and fit man who's available to carry them into the clean room so the women there can bag and tag."

After signing his time card, he walked to his locker in the

corner of the office. There, he removed his heavy coat and watch. Then he grabbed one of the company shirts and went into the employees' area to change.

Outside on the loading dock was a large truck with the back open. Scattered around were four or five men, a good dozen large cardboard boxes, and various coats and sweaters tossed against the wall.

"Neil!" Jerry called out. "Good to see you! How did you know to come in early? Did the boss give you a call?"

"Nope, I just thought I'd see if you needed help."

"We needed help about two hours ago." Wiping his brow, he added, "It's been slow going and hard work, too. I hate sweating in the winter."

"I was just thinking that same thing," he joked. As he pulled on his gloves, he looked around. "Where do you need me?"

"Out here on the loading docks. Put on a back brace and help us load boxes onto the dolly," another guy said. "This truck is packed and we haven't even gotten halfway through."

Though Neil didn't need a back brace, he put one on, then stepped into the truck. The moment he carried the full weight of one of the containers and slid it toward the ramp, his muscles clenched and burned.

And at that moment, he welcomed the pain. This was something normal and clean. It was something anyone could relate to and had nothing to do with regrets and hurts, uncles, fathers, or pretty girls with tear-filled eyes.

CHAPTER 25

Christmas was just around the corner. Planning for their first holiday in their new home was presenting everyone in Amanda's family with a welcome break from the stress surrounding the fire. Susanna had finished her Mason jars and they were now for sale in several stores in the area. Mamm had ordered a ham and, for their Christmas dinner, was making a new table runner. Amanda had been sewing her little crafts and helping her mother finish a quilt for a cousin.

She had also been speaking to more people about babysitting. She wanted to have a couple of jobs lined up in January. That would be a wonderful way to start the new year, she thought.

Because of her plans, she'd jumped at the opportunity to meet with an English couple at Bill's Diner to discuss a part-time nanny position.

When Traci had asked to accompany her, Amanda had thought it would do them both a lot of good. Traci had been so patient while recovering from her fall and cold. And Amanda still wasn't eager to go anywhere in Horse Cave completely by herself.

"Are you worried about meeting the family who asked you to be their nanny, Amanda?" Traci asked as they walked through the field toward the Kaufmanns' house.

"Of course not. I've babysat for lots of families over the years. I enjoy it. Plus, I'm anxious to earn a little extra money this winter."

Traci's hands were snuggling in her thick wool muff as she nodded. "I wish I had some extra money for gifts right now. All I've done is make coloring books for everyone."

"You are a talented artist. Everyone is going to enjoy your pages. It's a wonderful-*gut* gift to give to us all."

"Even Daed?" Traci asked.

Amanda laughed. "You've got me there. Even I can't see our father relaxing enough to spend a Sunday afternoon coloring pages."

"Me, neither." She sighed. "Susanna said since I helped her fill those jars and decorate them, she'd pay me when she gets paid."

"I'm sure she will."

"Maybe, but that didn't seem right," Traci said around another sigh. "This is her project. She should keep all her money, not be passing it to her little sister."

"You shouldn't think about it that way. Susanna has been working hard, but you helped her."

"I suppose." As they continued through the field, Traci pointed out a hawk flying overhead and a pair of deer contentedly eating winter grass in the distance.

Amanda loved walks like this. It made her feel like she

was taking the time to enjoy the Lord's blessings instead of merely rushing to get from one place to the other. She was thankful that her little sister seemed to be of the same mind.

Just as she was about to call attention to a redheaded woodpecker perching on a fence, Traci pointed over Amanda's shoulder. "Look, Manda. There is the Kaufmanns' *haus*."

"Yes, it is."

"I don't see anyone outside. Doesn't that surprise you?"

"A little bit, given that they have such a large family." Hoping she wasn't being too obvious, Amanda scanned the yard, hoping to "accidentally" spy Dale. However, Traci had been exactly right. No one was outside. No doubt that family was as busy as hers was, getting ready for the approaching holiday.

"They were sure nice when we went over there. And when they came over to our house to help clean up after the fire."

"I agree."

As they walked along, Traci glanced at the house again. "They sure got a lot of kids. Mamm said she doesn't know how Mrs. Kaufmann does it."

Amanda laughed. "Did you talk to Jimmy much when we were there?"

"*Nee*. Why?"

"Dale told me that he is thirteen years old, just like you. Maybe the two of you will become good friends."

Traci grunted. "I don't think so."

"Because?"

"Because he's a boy, Manda. And don't you start telling me about you and Dale, because we both know that's different."

"You are right," she said softly as she thought about how

much she'd enjoyed being in Dale's arms just the day before. "That is different."

"Do you think you're going to marry him one day?"

Last night when she'd gone to bed, Amanda had prayed about that very thing. Even though they'd just started courting, there seemed to be something between them that was special.

It was far too soon to speak about it with her sister, though. "Time will tell," she murmured as they continued on the path. The curved bridge was just up ahead. She had already decided to direct Traci over to the shallow place where Dale had helped her cross days ago. She had been afraid, but it was far safer than chancing the boards on the bridge.

Traci did not look impressed. "That's what Mamm says."

She chuckled. "Don't tell Mamm I said that, okay? I don't want her to know I'm already quoting her."

"Don't worry. Oh, Manda, look!"

Concerned, Amanda stared at the bridge, wondering if Traci was scared of it. "Dear, we're not going to step one foot on it. Instead—"

"*Nee*, look," she said again as she rushed toward the bridge.

As Amanda followed, she finally noticed what her little sister had been talking about. Someone had not only fixed the board that had broken when Traci had fallen, but had replaced another five or six. The new wood's pale color practically glistened compared to the other pieces of aged wood in the structure. "Someone repaired it already. It looks to be in good shape now, don't it?"

"Who do you think repaired it?"

"I'm sure it was Dale or someone in his family. Remember, the bridge is half theirs."

Some of the wariness in Traci's eyes eased. "Oh. Did he tell you that they repaired it yesterday?"

"*Nee*, but I'm sure they forgot with all the commotion about the fire."

She stopped at the beginning of the little bridge, her hand clasping one of the posts in a death grip. "I guess we should go over it, then."

Truthfully, Amanda was feeling a bit of foreboding, too. But surely she was letting her imagination get the best of her. "Want to go over it together?"

Traci took one step forward, now both of her hands clasping the railing on either side. "Maybe we should go one at a time. Just in case both of our weights are too much?"

Amanda swallowed and pasted yet another too-happy smile on her face. "That's a good idea. Do you want me to go first?"

"*Nee*. I'm already on it."

"Then cross whenever you are ready, dear," she said gently.

Looking more determined than ever, Traci stepped forward, slowly walking over the expanse. When she got to the other side, she exhaled loudly.

Amanda did the same.

As she crossed, a sudden burst of anger suffused her. This bridge was nothing. She and Traci should be walking over it without a second's thought. Yet, here they were, worrying about every little piece of wood.

It was so wrong.

When she got to the other side, she held out her hand. "We did it!"

Traci was beaming. "I can't wait to tell everyone that the bridge is as good as new."

"Better than that, even," Amanda declared as they made their way toward the main road.

Obviously happy to have that event behind her, Traci started chattering away, telling Amanda about books she read and a special fluffy robe she had hinted to their mother that she wanted for Christmas.

Amanda smiled, listened as best she could, and made all the appropriate responses. But her mind kept drifting back to Dale and her upcoming interview.

And then her heart practically stopped when she saw a man in the distance watching them. His arms were crossed and he had on a black hat like most Amish men wore in the winter.

He seemed slighter than Dale. He definitely had a slimmer build than Neil Vance.

Traci's voice drifted off as she noticed him, too. "Is that Dale?"

"*Nee.*"

"Who could it be, then?"

"I don't know."

"Why do you think he's just standing there?" Traci asked, her voice turning more wary. "Why is he watching us?"

"He might be taking a break or something," Amanda replied, but even to her ears the answer sounded weak. "Don't forget, we actually don't know too many people around here. He might take walks out here all the time."

"That's the difference between here and back home, isn't it?" Traci asked. "Back in Berlin, we knew everyone for miles and miles. Here, we hardly know anyone, but they all know us."

A chill ran down Amanda's spine as she considered her

sister's words. "Let's go, Traci," she said, picking up her pace. "I don't want to be late."

AN HOUR LATER, things seemed brighter, indeed. Mr. and Mrs. Parker had been so nice. When they first walked into Bill's, Amanda was charmed: Mr. Parker was carrying an infant carrier; and Mrs. Parker, a pink-striped tote bag filled with enough baby clothes, bottles, toys, and diapers to take care of their tiny baby girl for several days.

Later, when she got to hold two-month-old Pippin, she'd sighed in contentment. She so loved babies.

Mr. and Mrs. Parker had been sweet to Traci and had bought them all lunch. They had lists of questions, but as soon as they saw how easily Amanda cared for Pippin in her arms, all they wanted to do was schedule a first session.

To celebrate, Amanda took Traci to Horse Cave Salvage to do some shopping. While Amanda picked up some items for their mother, she gave Traci a couple of dollars to buy fried pies at the Amish bakery in the back of the large store.

Just as Traci bit into a cherry pie, they saw Neil Vance coming out of one of the back rooms. The moment he spied them, he walked over to say hello.

"This is a nice surprise. Did you come in for pies?" he asked after they all greeted each other.

"We came inside to celebrate," Traci said.

When Neil looked completely confused, Amanda laughed. "What she meant is that we came in so Traci could enjoy a fried pie."

"Not you, too?"

"After our big lunch, I canna eat another thing."

Neil winked at Traci. "I don't know about you, but I can always find room for cherry pie."

"Me, too," Traci said around a giggle.

As Amanda eyed Neil, she reflected that he seemed much more at ease and warm around them. Since she knew Susanna really liked him, she was glad about that. "How is work going?" she asked.

"It's all right. I came in early, so I'm almost done for the day. Um, how is Susanna?"

"She is *gut*. She's at home, helping our mother around the house," said Amanda.

"I hope things aren't in too much disarray after the fire?"

"Not too much. Luckily, we didn't have anything stored in the shed. We're shaken up, but we'll survive."

He smiled. Cleared his throat. "I'm glad to see you both. Now I can let you know that my family is planning to come over to see yours this evening."

"Tonight?" Amanda hoped she didn't sound as alarmed as she felt. "Is something wrong?"

"*Nee*. It's just . . . Well, I think we're all feeling terrible about the fire. And the other things that have been happening to you. My mother thought it was time to lend our support."

"That is kind."

"So, you don't think it would be a problem if we stopped over, unannounced?"

"Of course not," Traci said with a grin. "Susanna is going to be so happy," she continued in a singsong voice.

Amanda felt her cheeks heat. If Susanna heard Traci, she would be so embarrassed! "Traci is right, we'll look forward to seeing you tonight. And consider yourself announced. I'll tell my parents."

Neil looked relieved. "*Danke*. Well, I'll be seeing you, then." After sharing another smile with Traci, he turned and walked down an aisle.

The moment he was out of sight, Amanda stuffed the rest of Traci's fried pie back in her white paper sack. "You can finish this later. We've got to go."

Luckily, Traci didn't argue. After swiping her mouth with a paper napkin, she looked up at Amanda. "What do you think Susanna is going to say?"

"I don't know, but I do know what Mamm will say," she said as she grabbed her paper sack of groceries and shuttled her little sister back outside. "She's going to wonder why we didn't say no."

"Because she doesn't like Neil's family?" Traci asked with a frown.

Amanda laughed. "*Nee*, silly. Because she's not going to have enough time to bake two pies and a cake for them."

CHAPTER 26

Saturday, December 23

Iwould have preferred to have had more than one hour's notice that we would be having company tonight," Susanna's
mother chided as she moved around the kitchen like a nervous hummingbird. "You should have told me that Neil Vance
and his family were coming over the minute you found out,
Amanda."

After giving Susanna a look that said she was really, really
trying hard to keep her patience, Amanda replied, "I couldn't
very well do that, since we were in town picking up groceries
from Horse Cave Salvage. Traci and I still had to come all the
way home first."

"And don't forget that we told you as soon as we got here,"
Traci interjected. "So I don't think you should be upset with us."

Mother whirled on her. "Are you correcting me, Traci?"

She immediately shook her head. *"Nee."*

Pulling out a box of crackers, Mamm tore open the plastic
liner and began arranging them in neat rows on one of her
best platters. "I hope not."

Traci frowned, and when she folded her arms over her chest and looked like she was about to say something more, Susanna shook her head at her. "*Hush*," she mouthed.

Pulling out a container of cheese, Mamm glared. "I saw that, Susanna."

"Mother, why don't I arrange the cheese on the platter for you? While I'm doing that, Traci can pour some spiced pecans into bowls and Amanda can finish the coffee service."

"That ain't enough to serve them."

When Amanda sighed, which made their mother tense up even further, Susanna realized that they needed some help settling their mother down. "Where is Daed?"

"I sent him outside to sweep the front porch."

"He's been out there for quite some time, too. No doubt enjoying the peace and calm."

"Amanda, what is that supposed to mean?"

"Nothing, Mamm. Um, you know what? I think I should go check on Daed. Maybe he needs some help." Amanda smiled sweetly at Susanna as she made her escape.

"She did that on purpose," Traci whispered.

Susanna winked at her. Her sister was definitely not wrong. "Mother, you need to calm down. You are making us all nervous wrecks. The house is fine. It's all sparkling clean, too."

"But we hardly have any furniture. They'll think it looks bad."

"We just moved in," Susanna soothed. "No one will expect everything to look perfect."

"Perhaps not. I just don't know why they are stopping by," she said as the front door opened and Daed and Amanda came inside.

"Neil said he wanted to see Susanna," Traci called out from

the dining room, where she was staring out the window. "And he said that his parents felt real bad about the fire."

"There has to be another reason for their visit," Mamm murmured as she stared out the kitchen window. "Maybe they blame us?"

"For the fire?" Daed scoffed as he came inside. Wrapping an arm around her shoulders, he lowered his voice. "Don't start begging for trouble, Leah. It ain't helpful."

For the first time that hour, their mother seemed to relax. "You're right. I just wish I'd had time to make a cake or something."

"Next time they visit, you can."

"They're here!" Traci said from her spot at the window. "Susanna, you should open the door."

"Because?"

"Because he is your sweetheart," she said.

Susanna would have done something really mature and grown-up, like stick her tongue out at her, but her mother's chuckle was too good to hear.

She was still smiling about that when she opened the door to see Neil, a man who had to be his brother, and his mother. His father wasn't anywhere in sight. "*Wilcom*," she said, feeling a bit ironic. Honestly, she wasn't sure if his family was welcome or not.

Or, judging by the hesitant expressions on their faces, their guests weren't even sure that they wanted to be welcomed into their old house.

But Neil, as usual, handled everything in a level-headed way. "Susanna. Good evening. I hope our being here on the spur of the moment didn't cause you too much trouble."

"Of course not," she lied. "Please come in."

As her family crowded behind her, she introduced everyone. "I'm Susanna, these are my parents, John and Leah, and my two sisters, Amanda and Traci."

The younger boy held out his hand. "I'm Roy. It's *gut* to meet you. This is my mother, Johanna."

Shaking Roy's hand, she noticed that he looked much different than Neil. Oh, they had the same coloring, but their whole demeanors were different. Roy seemed to be as open and bright as Neil was closed and quiet.

"Won't you come in?" her mother said, her voice sounding strained.

"*Danke*," Johanna said. "But first, let me explain things a bit more. We wanted to come to let you know that we want to help you, not judge. I think we got off on the wrong foot and I'm embarrassed about that. Though we can't take back the past, I wish we could take back the way we handled this house's sale and our move." Lifting up a colorful gift bag, she said, "It's a small gesture, but I brought some pumpkin bread."

"It's still warm," Roy said with a grin. "That's why we were a little late. My mother insisted on making something fresh to bring over."

"We had to clean like crazy," Traci said.

Mamm winced. "Traci. Everyone, I'm sorry . . ."

"You know what? How about we all stop apologizing to each other?" Daed interjected smoothly. "I learned years ago that we're all just people in training, ain't so? We yearn to do things perfectly, but it's a hopeless cause."

Neil smiled at him, warmth lighting his eyes. "I like how you phrased that."

As her mother led everyone into the family room, an almost collective sigh occurred. Noticing that Neil had moved to her side, Susanna smiled at him. "So far, so good."

"It sounds like your mother was as *naerfich* as mine was."

"It's been eventful, but I'm glad you are here."

"Me, too," he said as they took the last two chairs.

Susanna noticed that her mother and Johanna Vance were already passing out coffee and serving warm pumpkin bread. Since Traci had already been put into service helping, Susanna simply relaxed next to Neil.

"Did you go over the reconstructed bridge?" Amanda asked.

Roy looked at her curiously. "What bridge are you talking about?"

"The one that was broken by the Kaufmanns' home."

"*Was* broken?" Roy asked. He looked at Neil. "I thought Dale was going to ask us to help him fix it this weekend."

"I thought so, too," Neil said.

"So he didn't tell you he fixed it?"

Looking confused, Neil shook his head. "*Nee*, but maybe he worked on it with his brother or something."

Amanda leaned back in her chair. "That's what I told Traci."

When Mrs. Vance sat down, she looked at them all again. "I need to apologize for my husband's absence. He was going to be here, coming here was actually his idea. But he, ah, said he had to do something with his brother. He said it couldn't wait."

"Of course. It's a busy time of year," Daed said. "And I know as well as anyone that horses and livestock don't care about what time of day it is."

Neil chuckled. "You are right about that. I've spent many a night nursing a horse or cow through a tough spot."

Now that the talk was in familiar territory, everyone seemed to relax. The Vances ate some pecans and crackers. Traci fetched Roy and Amanda glasses of water. Mamm stopped worrying and became her usual chatty self.

The conversation meandered from one topic to the next. Eventually Roy, Mr. Schwartz, and Traci were talking, while their mothers and Amanda chatted as well.

It was painfully obvious that everyone wanted to give Neil and Susanna a few minutes of privacy.

"I guess we've been granted their seal of approval," Neil said.

Susanna felt her cheeks heat. "Your brother and mother are nice."

"So, will you come over soon and bake with my mother?"

"We've already made plans while you were talking alfalfa with my father. I'm coming over tomorrow."

"On Christmas Eve."

"Yes. To help bake cookies . . . and deliver them."

"We can do that together. If it snows, we'll take a sleigh. If it's clear, we'll simply pull a wagon."

"I'm looking forward to it."

Finally, they had plans that had nothing to do with emergencies or trouble! His mother seemed to like her! Things were going to be just fine now.

That made her so happy, she could hardly do anything but smile. Luckily, her lack of conversation didn't seem to bother Neil any. He seemed content to simply sit with her and smile, too.

CHAPTER 27

Sunday, December 24

Couldn't you have made just a few dozen less cookies with my mother?" Neil asked as they walked down his driveway, an ancient red children's wagon trailing behind him.

Loaded in the wagon were at least two dozen brightly colored metal tins filled with all the Christmas cookies that she had made with Neil's mother. After they were cool, Susanna helped her fill the tins, tie ribbon around each one, and attach the gift tags.

Susanna chuckled. "I would have liked to have seen you tell her no. Your mother is a regular Christmas cookie–making machine! I was simply trying to keep up and be helpful."

"You were more than simply helpful. I know she enjoyed spending the day with you." His gaze turned more serious. "Just as I am looking forward to spending this afternoon and evening with you."

Gazing up into his blue eyes, Susanna felt a little burst of attraction and awareness. She had been looking forward to spending time with him, too. It seemed Neil Vance was all she could ever think about.

"I'm glad you took the day off. *Danke*."

"Don't thank me for this, Susanna. I wanted to be with you."

She gulped. Little by little, she had become used to Neil's serious ways. He wasn't a man who teased or joked all that much. He also didn't shy away from saying what was in his heart or on his mind. At first, his forthrightness had taken her aback. He was so different from every other man she'd known. His personality was even very different from his best friend's.

But now that she was used to it, Susanna was finding his personality rather comfortable. There was no guessing about what Neil was thinking.

That didn't mean, however, that she always knew how to respond. This was one of those moments. Instead of floundering or saying something silly, she kept her mouth shut and smiled.

"Too much?" he asked.

"*Nee*. I like how open and honest you are. But I am still learning how to respond in kind."

"There is no need for that. I don't want you to change."

She chuckled again. "Neil, I never know what to say when you say things like that." When he looked flustered, she raised her hand to the soft flakes that were swirling in the air around them. "Isn't it pretty out? Now it finally feels like Christmas is here."

"I like the snow, too. We actually haven't had too many white Christmases here. I bet you have, though."

"We have. I enjoy a snowy, white Christmas. It makes everything look so pure and perfect. I guess you could say it goes with the season's feeling of hope." She opened her mouth to mention how living in a big farmhouse this year was such a blessing and a dream fulfilled for her family, but of course she didn't want to be rude enough to share that.

As if he sensed her new tension, he looked down at her. "You know what? The Lord has given us an amazing surprise this year."

"Oh? What is that?"

"Now that the burdens of my father's debts are behind us and we aren't trying to figure out what to do, a new sense of peace has settled in our home. We are much more hopeful than we have been in years."

"Truly?"

He nodded, his expression as serious as always. "Stripping away all of our worries allowed us to concentrate on what is really important. Our faith, our health, our friends, and our loved ones."

"Maybe that is what Christmas is, then. It isn't looking forward to gifts we hope to receive, but cherishing those gifts we already have."

"I couldn't have said that any better," he said as they stopped in front of a row of duplexes. "Here's our first stop. Grab a tin and follow me."

Susanna did as he asked, even taking his hand as he led her up a row of cement steps that had never been shoveled.

When he knocked on the black door, an elderly Amish lady opened it warily, then smiled in pleasure when she spied Neil. "I didn't think I was going to see you this year, Neil."

"I wouldn't miss the opportunity to stop by, Emma. Merry Christmas." As he handed her a tin, he said, "Have you met Susanna yet?"

Emma held out her hand. "I heard rumors that the two of you are courting. I'm glad they were true."

Though it seemed too early to admit their relationship so publicly, Susanna knew it would be rude not to accept her kind remark graciously. "*Danke*. It's nice to meet you. Merry Christmas."

"Would you like to come in?"

"*Danke*, but we have a full wagon of cookies to deliver for my *mamm*. I would like to clear off your steps, though."

"I couldn't ask you to do that."

"You didn't ask, I offered." He raised his eyebrows. "Ain't so?"

When Emma still hesitated, Susanna smiled. "I've learned that it's sometimes easier to give Neil his way, Emma."

Walking to a closet, Emma pulled out a small silver snow shovel. "He's always been a stubborn man. But kind, too. *Danke*, Neil," she said.

As Neil began competently shoveling her narrow walkway and steps, Susanna chatted about the pretty weather and cookies. Then, in no time, they were saying good-bye and walking back to the wagon.

"Okay?" he murmured.

She knew what he was asking. Was she okay with visiting a bunch of people she didn't know, delivering cookies, and sometimes waiting while he did a small chore? "I'm *gut*."

He looked pleased as he picked up the handle. "The next *haus* is just up the street."

Over the next two hours, Susanna walked by his side and did almost the same thing as she'd done with Emma. She smiled when men and women mentioned that they were sweethearts, then stood while Neil shoveled sidewalks, picked up firewood, and even walked a dog.

At first, she'd been amazed about the audacity of people accepting Neil's offer. But then, she began to realize that they'd come to expect such small tasks from Neil. To refuse his offer would be as rude as not accepting the cookies that his mother had made them.

By the sixth house she began to realize she didn't just like Neil, she was falling in love with him. What other type of man would easily give so much without any expectation of thanks or his gift being reciprocated?

Realizing the season they were celebrating, she whimsically amended her thoughts. *Well, other than Jesus?*

After the twelfth stop, where she'd helped a young mother by playing with her toddler while Neil took out her trash, Susanna was beginning to feel tired. She had a pleasant ache in her bones that came from being busy on her feet all day.

Neil was looking a little weary, too. "Only one more stop to go, Sue," he said. "Then, how about we head over to Bill's Diner and have supper out?"

"I can't think of anything I'd rather do."

He grinned. "Me, neither."

They were walking near the center of Horse Cave, and just a block away was the entrance to the cave. The snow was coming down good now that darkness had fallen. The ticket office was closed. Most of the stores were locked for the night, and it had even been a few minutes since they'd seen a vehicle on the road. It was peaceful. She could hear the crunch of their boots on the freshly fallen snow and the low screech of the wagon's tires as it trailed behind them.

"Here's the last house," Neil said, pointing to a small, dark building just off the main road.

"I didn't know anyone lived there." Every time she'd gone

by the old place, she'd noticed that the yard was full of debris and equipment that had been neglected or forgotten. "Actually, I think this is the first time I've ever seen it lit up the way it is."

"You know what? Me, too."

"Maybe she saw us walking and lit some lamps for us."

"Maybe, but that don't really sound like her."

"Oh?"

"The woman who lives here? Her name is Velma. She's a widow. She ain't all that nice, I'm afraid." He sighed. "I don't know if it's because she's ailing or that she simply doesn't care, but she, um, she's also rather unkempt. She's not only grumpy but usually kind of smells. She also, well, loves to give me work."

Why did that not surprise her? Realizing that she was being uncharitable, she murmured, "It's so kind of you to do this."

He pulled at his collar. "I'm ashamed to say that sometimes my stop here feels more like an obligation than an act of kindness. Sue, I fear you're going to be gritting your teeth by the time I finish with whatever chore she gives me."

In no hurry to stand in the cold and talk to a cranky old woman, Susanna smiled at him. "Maybe I could help pick up some of these items in her yard instead of talking?"

"If she lets you, I think that would be a fine idea. It would be a little warmer, too. This wind is sinking into my bones. Let's hope and pray that Velma is both more conciliatory and quick about choosing my chore for her than in years past."

Neil's quip sounded so different than his usual way of talking about people that Susanna simply smiled and followed him down the small dip toward the house.

"Careful here, Sue. It can be real slick."

Just as she was about to acknowledge his comment, she stumbled. "Oh!" she called out as her feet slipped out from under her. "You weren't kidding."

He knelt by her side. "I wasn't, but I didn't want you hurt. You all—"

But then her stomach dropped as the surface they were on suddenly gave way underneath them.

She screamed as she plunged down into darkness.

CHAPTER 28

Sunday, December 24

The first thing Neil noticed was the smell. Mildew and musk. Mud and decay. That, combined with the damp chill and the faint sound of trickling water, left him no doubt as to what had happened. They hadn't fallen down an abandoned mine shaft.

Instead, they had landed somewhere far more dangerous. They were somewhere in Horse Cave.

Somehow, they'd fallen down a boarded-up old entrance to the cave. There weren't lots of old entrances around the area, but there were more than two or three. Most were well marked with NO TRESPASSING signs. Some had even been covered with old stone or cement over the years.

Others had not.

He vaguely remembered his father and uncle telling him and Roy scary ghost stories about falling into the cave if they weren't careful. He and Roy had listened to the stories with wide eyes, shivering as their imaginations took flight. Roy had been scared of the nests of bats he was sure populated the cave.

Neil's own worries had been more rooted in reality. Everyone knew that the cave could fill up with water in minutes, drowning all the inhabitants inside.

There had been a glimmer of truth to the tales, which had made the stories seem even more disturbing. Growing up, he and Roy had heard a multitude of stories about how earlier residents of the area used to be quite the entrepreneurs.

After Mammoth Cave had been discovered and the rest of the county had become "cave crazy," many residents set up their own travel industry. They'd hastily cleaned out one of the many entrances to the spidery underground caverns, making a slipshod entrance and charging a couple of bits to interested tourists.

But unlike some of the other caverns in the area, Horse Cave had a tendency to flood. When a couple of locals died, most of the tourism boom had dried up.

The townspeople had then moved on to other venues, hastily boarding up the old entrances before moving on. When the Commonwealth took over the running of Horse Cave, a couple of men had been paid to carefully seal the other entrances. But outsiders would never know all the entrances, mainly because there were still enough residents who didn't trust outsiders on their property.

Therefore, it was a common joke that longtime members of the community could slip in and out of the caves undetected, if that was what they desired.

Neil figured few people ever did. The unexplored and narrow branches of the cave were treacherous and dark, susceptible to flash floods and even unfortunate receptacles to poor sewage systems.

So, Neil had known such entrances had existed, but he'd

thought the stories about simply falling through the ground into the vast cavern had been greatly exaggerated. He'd always thought the men had told those stories as a way of either scaring them at Halloween or to encourage them not to wander off when they were out walking. But it seemed like it hadn't been an old wives' tale after all.

Finally, clearing his head, he sat up, moaning under his breath as his body protested the movement. He experimentally shifted his limbs, wondering if he'd sprained or broken anything. But though he hurt, he was in good shape.

Until he realized that he hadn't heard anything besides the sound of water dripping around him.

"Susanna?" he called out. "Susanna, can you hear me?"

Silence.

He swiped at his eyes, struggled to discern any shape or movement in the dark. But though he was slowly able to distinguish various shades of gray, he couldn't see her form.

Worry turned to panic. What if she was grievously hurt? What if she'd hit her head and couldn't speak? How was he going to be able to get her help? *"Susanna?"* he called out again, this time even more loudly. *"Are you nearby? Can you say anything?"*

After a few seconds that felt like long hours, he heard a scramble followed by a faint moan.

Tears pricked his eyes, he was so relieved. "Sue, say something, okay? Say anything so I can help you."

"Neil?" She coughed, gasped. Then spoke again. "Neil, here I am. Can you see anything? I can't."

"I can't see much, but I think I'm near you. Sit tight, okay? I'll be there as soon as I can."

She laughed softly, the sound raw and ragged. "Don't worry. I'm too afraid to move."

She was to his right. Afraid to get to his feet in case they had landed on an even more precarious part of the cave than he'd imagined, he crawled toward her. The rock was cold and slick under his hands, coated with condensation and algae.

"So, I guess we're in the cave."

"*Jah.*"

She laughed softly. "I've been wanting to explore it, but I would've rather picked another way."

"And I would've rather taken you another time. Preferably in the summer and with some flashlights on hand," he said as he continued edging toward her voice.

"What do you think happened? One moment we were walking, the next, I woke up and you were calling my name."

She'd woken up. "Did you pass out? Did you hit your head?" he asked anxiously.

"I don't know. Maybe I just got the wind knocked out of me."

Neil knew she was nearby, though he was also pretty sure she was resting lower than he was. "Keep talking, Sue. I think you might be a little below me."

"Below you?" He heard her fumble around. "Eww. It is really wet around here."

"How wet? Most times there's a small rivulet of water down at the bottom. Do you think you landed in that?" Please, God, he hoped not. Because if she was that far down, then not only was he going to have to get down to her but he was also going to find a way to get himself and her back up.

"Um, let me see . . ." Her first words drifted off as he heard her shuffle around a bit.

"Be careful!"

"I am." After a couple more seconds of knocking, she moaned. "Well, there's good news and bad news."

In spite of himself, Neil smiled. Only Susanna could say things like that in such a scary situation. "Let's have the good news first."

"I don't think I'm in a creek bed or anything like that. The water is only a few inches deep. That's *gut, jah?*"

"*Jah.* That's wonderful-*gut.*" His right hand reached out, felt the edge of the ledge he now realized he was on. "I think I'm close, Susanna. Keep talking. Tell me your bad news."

"Well, I think I hurt my wrist. *Nee.* I know I hurt it." She let out a small groan. "I can hardly move it."

Inwardly, he cursed. That was bad news. If she only had one arm that she could use, then it was going to be even harder to pull her up. Struggling to keep his voice even, he said, "What about everything else?"

"Everything else?"

"*Jah.* Your back, your legs . . . can you move them?"

There was another pause as he imagined her moving her limbs experimentally. "I think so."

"That's *gut.*"

"Neil, what about you?"

"I'm all right." And because he heard the new thread of worry in her voice, he interjected a new note of confidence in his voice. "You know me. I'm too ornery for a little thing like a fall to hurt me."

As he'd hoped, she chuckled.

Shifting slightly, he stuck part of his right leg over the ledge, so he could swing the lower portion of his leg. "Susanna, I think I'm right above you. Now, I know it's dark, but I want you to try real hard to find my foot. I think it's swinging above you."

"I hear your voice, but I think you're quite a bit higher. Too far for me to reach you easily."

"That means you're going to have to climb to your feet and reach a hand up for my foot. Can you do that?"

She made a choking noise that sounded a lot like she was fighting back tears. "It's really dark. I canna even see my hand when it's in front of my face."

"I know. But you have to have faith, ain't so?"

"I know, but—"

"Susanna, can you feel for a wall or something? Use it to help yourself."

She was panting now. Verging on panic. Neil would've been tempted to try to encourage her, but he didn't know the right words to say. After all, what were the words? It was a scary thing to move around in a house when it was completely dark—in a cave, with water nearby, and when neither of them had any inkling of what was near them . . . ?

He figured it was verging on terrifying.

"I would give a lot right now to have on pants instead of this heavy cloak and dress."

"I'd tell you to take it off, but I fear you'd get too chilled."

"Neil, I can't believe you said that."

He smiled, because now there was a note of humor peeking through her tear-filled voice. "It's shocking, but it ain't like I could see ya. True?"

"Maybe." He heard a wet-sounding smack of her hand. "Oh! I found a wall."

Forcing himself not to add to her anxiety, he worked to keep his voice calm. "That's *gut*. Use it to help you get to your feet."

"Okay. Hold on. I don't know why, but I can't seem to talk to you and concentrate on getting to my feet at the same time."

"I understand."

"Do you?" she asked after a pause. Endless minutes passed as he heard her shuffling below him. With each shift he felt his worry for her increase. Dozens of things could go wrong and he'd have no way to help her.

At last, she spoke. "Okay, I'm on my feet now. Please, God, let you be close."

Her artless comment made him realize that he should have been praying. Quietly, he asked the Lord to be with her. To be with them.

"Neil?"

"What?"

"I'm looking for you. You've gotta keep talking."

He chuckled. "Sorry, I was just thinking I should start praying."

"You haven't started? Neil, all I've been doing is praying!"

That made him smile. "It's working, *jah*. You have made good progress."

"That's a good point," she said. "I'm going to have to start praying to get rescued quickly."

Her faith in the midst of their situation was inspiring. "Do you think He intends to answer our prayers?"

"I don't see why not. We are good people. And we are believers. Oh!"

"What?"

"Oh, I hit my arm on something. It really stung." Her breath hitched. "Okay, I'm taking another step toward you."

"I'll keep talking, then." Of course, now that it was his

turn to chatter on, his head felt like it was made of cotton. Why couldn't he focus?

Because he was afraid for her.

"Neil?"

"Sorry. I was, um . . . I was just thinking about you," he said at last.

"Me?"

"*Jah.* I, um, I was thinking about how glad I am to know you."

"I wouldn't have guessed you saying that. I haven't brought you anything but pain and trouble."

"That ain't true. You've been a lot of things to me. A lot of good things."

"Even if I have been, I'll never be able to return the favor. After all, you rescued me that night after Thanksgiving."

"Sometimes I think you've rescued me, too," he admitted. "Before we met, I was so consumed by pain and embarrassment that I had stopped feeling hopeful. You changed that."

"I had no idea."

"That's because I've been too afraid to tell you. But the truth? Well, the truth is that you arrived in my life like a gift."

"A gift? Really?"

Liking the comparison, he nodded, though of course she couldn't see him. "*Jah.* I thought you were a pretty girl, all wrapped up in dark hair and green eyes. But when I learned what you were like underneath all that pretty wrapping, well, it was a treasure I couldn't have imagined. You are positive and full of energy and a goodness that I'd forgotten was in me, too. I just want you to know that I'm grateful for you. I'm glad we've gotten to know each other."

"Me, too." She sighed. "Neil, I don't know what to do. I keep feeling around, but I—"

He felt her hand push his boot. "You found me."

She laughed. "I did, didn't I? Well, what do you think we should do now?"

"I'm going to help you get up near me. And then we're going to do the only thing we can. We're going to wait to be rescued," he said as confidently as he could.

Because inside? . . . Well, he had no idea if that was a possibility·or not.

CHAPTER 29

Sunday, December 24

Dale Kaufmann had almost gotten up the nerve to kiss Amanda when the double doors to the hearth room swung open and half his family strode in without a second's hesitation.

With a little squeal, Amanda pulled away from him on the couch. Blushing furiously, she pressed her palms to her cheeks.

"Don't worry, Manda," he said quietly before getting to his feet.

She averted her face. It was obvious that she wished she was absolutely anyplace else.

He knew the feeling.

Seeing as his eldest brother, who was practically married off, was in the lead, he unleashed his anger on him. "Max, haven't we moved on from these games?"

Max's eyes darted from Dale to Amanda, then back again. "Sorry to, uh, interrupt, Dale, but we've got a problem."

Right then he realized that not only were Max and Beth

in the room, but also his sister Esther and Neil's brother, Roy. Every one of them was staring at Amanda with concern. "What happened?"

"Amanda, there's no way to tell you this easily. Your sister and Neil Vance are missing."

While Dale felt his body stiffen with shock, she shook her head. "*Nee*, they aren't missing. They're delivering cookies for Mrs. Vance. I mean, for your mother, Roy."

"They did do that, but they left hours ago. They should have been back by now."

Her eyes widened. "Are you sure?"

Taking Amanda's hand, Dale said, "I bet they went to Bill's Diner or something. There ain't no reason to get everyone worried for nothing."

"Someone found the wagon Neil had been pushing and brought it to our house almost two hours ago," Roy said, his expression grim. "My mother, Daed, Uncle Joseph, and I went right out and started asking if anyone had seen them. The trail ended just off of Sixth Avenue."

"Your uncle?"

"*Jah*. It surprised me, too. But Joseph acted as if he was surprised that we didn't think he'd want to go."

Amanda squeezed Dale's hand. "Roy, where are my parents?"

"At your *haus*. My mother wanted to tell your mother right away."

"Our parents just went over there, too," Esther said. "They're going to come up with a search-party plan."

"I need to go home," Amanda said.

Dale gazed at her in concern. She was sounding shaky. "Of course you do," he said gently. "I'll walk you there right now."

Esther held out a hand for Amanda to take. "Let me help

you find your cloak and boots. With so many people in this house, everything gets lost or mixed up."

"All right," Amanda said. As she started following Esther, she looked over at Dale again, her blue eyes looking languid. She was close to tears. "Dale, you coming?"

He nodded. "I'll be right there. I promise, Manda."

"Come on, Amanda," Esther said kindly. "I promise, it's easier just to give Dale a moment to talk to the men. Then, he'll be along. I bet by the time we sort out all the boots."

When the girls were out of the room at last, Dale stared at Roy. "I hate that she's so scared. Are you sure about this? I know Neil almost as well as you do. He does everything slow and methodical. I can't imagine him deciding to take Susanna somewhere private and losing track of time."

"I'm sure." Lowering his voice, Roy said, "We have a pretty good idea about where the two of them vanished. Well, we've narrowed it down to two places."

"Where?"

Roy hesitated. "I think it would be better if you asked the sheriff or Deputy Beck that. They're already searching the area."

"The authorities are already involved?" Even he knew that most authorities wouldn't start searching for missing persons until they'd waited at least a couple of hours.

"After the deputy's wife got attacked last year, I don't think he's one for taking chances anymore." Roy shrugged. "I, for one, am really glad that they aren't wasting time. It's really cold out. The temperatures are supposed to be in the low twenties tonight."

"This news is getting worse and worse."

"*Jah*," Roy said around a sigh. "This has been one of the worst evenings of my life, for sure."

Dale stared at him closely. Of course Roy was going to be upset and anxious about his brother. That was to be expected. But Dale would bet a dollar that he was worried about something else, too. Roy's expression was too ravaged, his manner too tense. "Hey, are you all right?"

"Dale, come on, if you're coming," Esther called out.

"I want to talk to you, but I've got to go," he said. "I know Amanda's anxious to be with her parents."

"Of course she is." Roy stared at Dale a moment longer, then seemed to come to a decision. "If you don't mind, I think I'll go with you over to the Schwartzes' house."

"You are really worried about Neil and Susanna, aren't you?"

"I am. But to be honest, it's not just that." He swallowed hard. "I fear I know who is behind this."

"Really? Is it . . . Is it someone you know?"

He nodded. "Unfortunately, I fear it's someone I know very well."

CHAPTER 30

Sunday, December 24

At least two hours had passed since Neil had gripped her arms and helped her scrabble up the ledge to reach his side. It hadn't been easy. The walls of the cave were damp and slick, her dress and cloak were ungainly, and her left wrist and hand throbbed painfully.

She'd cried out in pain when he pulled, which she knew had made Neil feel worse. She'd felt terrible for not being able to hold back her cry and apologized several times.

He'd brushed off her worries, citing the obvious. She was injured and climbing up had made her hand hurt.

After Susanna had gotten up safely, they scooted back against the wall. They were sitting side by side. A little while ago, she clasped his arm tightly with her good hand, curving her body into his for added warmth. It was so very cold.

Neil had become even quieter. She knew he was worried about her and about how long the two of them would be able to manage before they were rescued.

She was worried about those things as well. She knew God

watched after His flock, and she knew He wouldn't have placed the two of them here in this cave without a good reason. But even knowing that didn't make their circumstances feel any easier.

"Do you think it's still snowing?" she asked after silently praying for help yet again.

"Hmm? Oh, well, *jah*. I mean, probably so," Neil replied, his distracted tone revealing that he, too, had been letting his mind drift. "The weather reports predicted it was going to snow through the night and give everyone a white Christmas."

"That will be something," she said, attempting to infuse a bit of excitement in her voice. "Ain't so?"

"*Jah*." He cleared his throat. "I'm sure it's going to look real pretty. My mother will be so pleased."

"My sister Traci will be excited about it, too." Though she doubted any member of her family was going to be thinking about the weather conditions if she and Neil weren't found. "Neil, if . . . if the snow continues to fall, all of our tracks will be covered up."

"I thought of that, too. But we left the wagon. Someone will see that."

"You're right." She tried to inject a note of optimism in her voice but feared she was failing miserably. "And surely someone will remember us pulling it. We went to a lot of houses."

"That is true. My mother has no doubt been telling everyone whose houses we were going to. I bet my father or Roy or any number of other people have gone to each one to see if we showed up. So, you see, it's only a matter of time before someone walks down that alleyway."

Unless no one was looking for them yet. Or, unless they

didn't see the wagon or didn't see where their weight broke through the old dilapidated entrance.

"I bet my parents or yours have already contacted Sheriff Brewer," she continued in her bright tone. "And I bet he's put Deputy Beck and everyone from the volunteer fire department on the streets."

He laughed, the noise echoing in the dark cave. "Maybe so."

As his laughter faded, new tension filled the air. Though she didn't want to borrow trouble, Susanna also didn't want to pretend the obvious couldn't be occurring. "Have you thought that maybe someone sabotaged that walkway on purpose?"

"Like someone knew we would be heading to that house?"

"*Jah.*"

He sighed. "I haven't wanted to believe it, but I think there really is someone who doesn't want your family living on that farm. Maybe he doesn't even want me there, either."

"But why? It's just land."

"It is just farmland to you. To me, it represents a legacy that I've always assumed I was going to inherit. Maybe it represents something else to whoever has been bothering your family."

She racked her brain, trying to think what that could be. Then she realized that there was no point in trying to discover a logical reason for someone to break bridges and fencing, shoot at her buggy, burn out buildings, and now trap them in a cave on Christmas Eve. She would have never done any of those things.

But someone had.

She was scared. She was frightened and cold and losing hope. Sometime soon, she knew she'd finally lose her battle to keep her tears at bay.

Only the fact that she wasn't sitting alone was keeping her from giving in to hysterics. She'd never been afraid of the dark, but this abandoned space they were perched on was giving new meaning to pitch-black.

Releasing a ragged breath, she tried to picture Neil. She knew he was sitting right next to her. His knees were pulled up in front of him, one of his arms resting on those knees. His other hand was curved around her knee. His scent, so clean and masculine, helped combat the mustiness and mildew that permeated the space.

Keeping that image in mind, she edged closer and tucked her hand around his arm. Maybe if she concentrated on how he felt and smelled she would be able to block out the musty, cold air that surrounded them.

"I ain't gonna ask if you're all right," Neil said after listening to her carry on for a while. "I know you're not."

And that was all she needed to send her over the edge. "I'm so sorry for all of this." Hearing her words, how useless and, well, pitiful they sounded, given the fact that they were stuck in a cave, she moaned softly. "But saying I'm sorry doesn't even cover it, does it?"

She felt him shift beside her. "Why do you need to apologize?"

"I don't know. Maybe if my family had never wanted to move here, your family wouldn't have moved and everything would still be okay."

"But it wouldn't. We had to find a buyer. If your family hadn't bought our farm, we would have sold it to someone else."

"Maybe."

"*Nee*. It is absolutely true, Susanna. My father owed the bank thousands of dollars. And my uncle was really being difficult. He was wanting to take over the land and eventually sell it to developers. My father wanted to sell it to someone who wanted to farm the land."

"Maybe I'm the target, then. If you hadn't been my friend, you wouldn't be here."

"Susanna, you need to stop thinking about what-ifs and what-might-have-beens. It serves no purpose and doesn't change the way things are."

"You are right. It is impossible to go back in time, I guess."

"It's not only impossible, I wouldn't want to. Everything that's happened before now has brought us to this place. And one day the two of us are going to understand why the Lord brought us here on Christmas Eve."

Even though he couldn't see, she nodded again. She did need to remember his words. That not only was this supposed to happen, that one day they would be just fine and this would be just a memory.

"This is going to sound crazy, but if the Lord really has decided that two people needed to be stuck in this cave tonight, I'm glad I'm with you."

"Neil. The things you say."

"It's true. I couldn't bear it if I knew you were alone down here."

"I'm glad you're here, too." She could almost feel him smile. She took comfort in that and snuggled closer to him. He lifted his arm and wrapped it around her shoulders. Now her head was resting on his chest. She couldn't hear his heartbeat through all the layers, but she could feel the firm muscles that lay underneath. She closed her eyes and breathed in his scent again. Tried to imagine that they were somewhere far different. Maybe in a buggy together. Maybe on a couch in a warm living room.

Minutes passed. She gave up straining to hear faint voices or footsteps. She stopped thinking about anything but him and how good it felt to be in his arms.

"Susanna, I've thought and thought, but I can't think of any way to get us out of here. If I had a flashlight, or even a book of matches, things would be different. But I don't. It's too dark to explore and try to find another way out. I don't want to risk leaving you alone, either."

She trembled. "I don't know if I could handle sitting here by myself for hours, Neil. I would be too worried about you."

"At least we're together."

Neil's voice, so thick with emotion, gave her a sense of warmth and security that she'd feared she would never have. How had he become so important to her?

"I used to be afraid of you," she blurted. In the enclosed space, the words reverberated, practically bouncing off the walls. Embarrassing her. Why in the world had she decided to admit it aloud?

Neil shifted. In her mind, she could see snippets of his face. His furrowed brows. His strong jaw. The faint scar on his left eyebrow. Finally, his light-blue eyes filled with emotion.

But though she could almost perfectly imagine how he was looking, she had no idea what he was thinking. Was he embarrassed? Angry? Amused?

If he was amused by her revelation, that would be so embarrassing. And given that they were stuck together? It would be practically a disaster, and probably no less than she deserved.

He coughed. Then, after a lengthy pause, he spoke. "I know you were. Part of me was a little glad about it, I think."

"Because you didn't like me."

"Because I didn't *want* to like you." He whistled low. "Shoot, I remember the first moment I saw you. You were lying on the ground, snow falling all around you, your lips slightly parted. I feared you were unconscious." He sighed. "*Nee*, that ain't true. I was afraid you were dead, Susanna. I feared you were dead or injured and that I wasn't going to be able to help you. But in the middle of all of that, I couldn't help but stare. I thought you were the prettiest thing I'd ever seen."

"You thought I was pretty. Lying there on the ground," she murmured.

"*Jah*. That's shameful. Ain't so?" He chuckled low. "I wish I could tell you how ashamed I am of myself. But I can't deny how I was feeling. Then, when you opened your eyes, they were so green. So perfectly green. Whew. I knew I was a goner."

"All I remember from that meeting was your deep voice. You sounded almost otherworldly. At first, I thought maybe I had died."

"And I was your angel? Hardly."

She chuckled. "I wasna afraid of you then, Neil. I was afraid of you when I realized who you were—and I saw how mad you were at me."

"I wasn't mad at you. I was mad at the situation. I thought that the Lord had played a cruel joke on me. I thought I had found a woman to spend the rest of my life with . . . when your being in my life symbolized everything that had gone so wrong. I had a difficult time putting our meeting and the loss of everything I thought I had known together."

His voice was hoarse, like it was pulling almost everything he had inside of him to share his innermost thoughts with her.

"When did you change your mind?"

He laughed. "Practically the first moment after we parted. I realized that pushing you away had not only caused you pain but hurt me, too. I wanted to get to know you better, you see."

"I had no idea."

"I'm glad about that. I was so confused! If you had understood how I was feeling better than I? Well, I would have been even more of an emotional mess."

Before she could even attempt to reply to that admission, he continued, his voice lowered. "Then there was Dale."

"Dale? What did he have to do with us?"

"He was my voice of reason. Oh, but he was upset that I had been so awful to you. When I tried to defend myself, he talked to me like only a good friend could. He said I was wrong and that I needed to apologize."

She smiled to herself, imagining what that conversation must have been like. "I'm guessing his words weren't easy to hear."

He chuckled softly. "Not in the least. But when I tried to defend myself again, I realized that I couldn't. And that's when I knew."

"That's when you knew you liked me?"

"Maybe, I don't know. All I do know is that I didn't need a reason to understand my feelings for you. I just did."

"And then?"

"And then I knew I wanted you to be mine one day," he said. "I know, right?" He laughed again, but the sound was still forced. Hollow sounding. "None of what I just said probably makes a bit of sense. It probably embarrasses you, too."

"*Nee*. I'm not embarrassed."

"I'm grateful for that, at least."

His words surprised her but weren't shocking. She was old enough to feel the tension that had blossomed between them. Old enough to notice when he'd gazed at her a little too long. She'd been aware that he sometimes reached out to assist her when she hadn't actually needed any help at all.

Susanna knew that the right thing to do would be to reveal how she felt about him as well. He'd taken a risk by being open and honest. To not respond in the same way was doing them both a disservice. But she wasn't quite ready.

It seemed even when she was trapped in a dark cavern and the chances of being rescued quickly were becoming less and less of a possibility, there were other things she feared almost as much. She was afraid to trust that what they had was real. From the moment their paths had crossed, they'd been caught up in a whirlwind of danger. How would a relationship born of such high drama and emotion survive when things settled down?

Did some relationships fail when there was nothing to keep emotions high? She didn't know.

Susanna worried, too, about being vulnerable. She didn't want to risk her heart. She didn't want to take a chance on giving him the one part of her that he could damage with just a few words or actions.

With all of that in mind, she focused on his words instead of what was in her heart. "During these last couple of weeks, I've thought a lot about your resentment of me."

"Susanna, *nee*." He sounded pained. "Didn't you hear what I said? I was wrong."

"No, listen to me. I realized that your family was hurting," she said at last. "I guess you needed an enemy. We provided that for you."

"That isn't something I'm proud of."

"There is nothing wrong with being human, Neil."

"Maybe not. But it was wrong for me to act so selfishly."

"Don't you think you're being a little hard on yourself?"

"*Nee.*"

"Neil!" Boy, she wished she could see his face. Baring one's soul in the dark was a difficult task. She felt like she was fumbling around in a closet, never picking out the right words to say.

"I mean, really, Susanna. Look at us now. Here we are, sitting together in the dark. You're hurt, it's cold, and our clothes are damp. Right now, we only have each other. We don't even have a match or water to drink."

"You're not helping me feel better," she teased.

"I know. But what I'm saying is that right now, when we have so little, I can hardly believe how I acted, as if I deserved more than I was ever given, as if no one else had ever had their financial situations change. It was wrong of me."

Before she could comment on that, he reached for her hands. "When I heard your buggy crash, I ran across the woods to help you. I prayed that you would survive."

She squeezed his hands, hoping to convey with her touch how much she appreciated his actions. "You did help me survive. If not for you, I might have died, or at least been a lot worse off. I will always be grateful for you."

"I know. But will you always be glad that I turned on you so quickly? Practically the moment I realized who you were, I turned away."

"All that is behind us now."

"*Jah.* I suppose it is."

As the silence stretched between them, Susanna knew

there was no better time to share what was in her heart. Gathering her courage, she licked her bottom lip. "Can I tell you something else? Something that I don't think I would tell you if we weren't sitting here in the dark?"

"You can tell me anything you want."

She pulled back her hands, almost afraid to give him both her hands and her heart. "I, well, I think I've fallen in love with you."

She heard his breath hitch. Felt his body tighten as he moved closer and reached for her hands again.

Waiting for his response, she tried to regret being so impulsive. But she couldn't. She wouldn't allow herself to be sorry. If this was the last night they had together, she wanted it to be filled with honesty.

After rubbing a thumb over her knuckles, he shifted his hands, linking their fingers together. "I've fallen in love with you, too, Susanna."

"Really?" she asked hesitantly. "You aren't just saying it because I did?"

"I think you know I'm not the kind of man to say or do anything that I don't mean."

"No, I suppose you aren't."

"And this is a place for honesty, don't you think?"

"Yes. That was why I told you what was in my heart. When we've practically lost everything else? I think only honesty matters."

"If we get out of here—" He stopped. "*Nee*. I mean, *when* we get out of here, I'm going to talk to your parents. I want to gain their permission and marry you as soon as we can."

"Neil!"

"No, don't say it's too much or too sudden. If tonight has

taught me anything, it's that I don't want to spend so much time worrying about what people think or how they might react."

Joy bubbled through her. She'd found joy, here in one of the darkest places she'd ever been. The Lord was showing her that light could shine in almost every corner of the world.

CHAPTER 31

Monday, December 25

"No matter what happens, or what people think, you need to tell Sheriff Brewer your suspicions, Roy," Dale said as dawn broke on Christmas Day.

They'd been together all through the night. A whole group of them had gathered at Joseph Vance's house. At first, Dale had thought it had been an unlikely choice for the sheriff to set up the base, but in the end it had seemed the right one. Joseph had the space for dozens of people to congregate while forming search parties or sitting together to talk or to pray.

Everyone had also realized that the Schwartz family was in no position to be in any kind of leadership role. They were scared and frightened and had appeared more than a little shell-shocked about the whole situation. Not a single person blamed them. The Schwartzes didn't know many people in the area, and certainly knew of no places where Neil and Susanna could have been.

Joseph, on the other hand, had seemed to be at his best. He'd tirelessly worked with the law enforcement officials, his brother's family, and everyone who had stopped by with food, blankets, and helping hands. He'd given directions and his opinion in a calm and frank manner and seemed to also know when it was time to step back and simply listen.

They'd had search parties out until almost eleven at night. It was obvious to everyone that no progress was going to be able to be made until dawn broke.

The Schwartzes took over two of Joseph's bedrooms. Neil's parents had gone home. Roy, Dale's entire family, and about a dozen other folks had simply fallen into an exhausted slumber in the early hours of the morning in Joseph's large living room.

When dawn broke, Sheriff Brewer and Deputy Beck returned with several other officers on loan from neighboring towns. They were outside on the front porch poring over maps.

Dale and Roy were standing just on the other side of the front door, watching them.

And, in Roy's case, debating about what to do next. "If I share my suspicions, it's going to change my life." Wearily, he rubbed the dark smudges under his eyes. "I've been praying all night. Asking God to tell me what to do. Even asking God to reassure me that it would be better to keep my suspicions to myself."

"But He hasn't done that?"

He shook his head. "I don't think so." Looking around the house's entryway, Roy said, "Actually, I think He has been giving me a reason to share."

"If you know anything that can help, you need to say it, Roy. This isn't about you or me."

Staring out the window, he nodded. But still he didn't move.

The tension and the gravity of the situation had finally taken its toll. Dale felt his temper snap. "This is your brother we are talking about. He could be hurt. He could be dying. And Susanna Schwartz is with him. She is with Neil because your family delivers gifts every year to people in need. She never would have been out on Christmas Eve if not for that."

"I know. Believe me, I know."

"Then what loyalty could you possibly have that is more important than that?"

Instead of answering, Roy pulled back his shoulders, yanked open the front door, and strode out to Sheriff Brewer.

Through the window, Dale watched him say something to the sheriff. The sheriff paused, then after speaking to Deputy Beck, he walked Roy to the other side of the front porch. It was obvious, to Dale at least, that Roy had asked to speak to the sheriff in private.

As he watched, the sheriff's expression went from confused to incredulous to intent. Then he called Deputy Beck over.

When Roy spoke again, he looked visibly upset. But his chin was lifted and he was looking directly into the sheriff's eyes. Whatever Roy was saying, it was evident that he was sure about it.

It seemed Roy had made the right call.

Feeling the first glimmer of hope in several hours, Dale went in search of Amanda. He was so worried about her and her family. They looked to be hanging on to their hope and composure by the thinnest thread.

She'd told him sometime in the middle of the night about how sick her mother had been. How she was still not as strong as she should be. Though her father was standing strong, he was worried about his daughter. And then there was Traci, who'd looked so lost from the moment she'd first heard the news.

Last night, he'd tried his best to comfort Amanda and give her the support she needed, but he knew that Neil's and Susanna's fates were not in his hands. Their futures were now only in God's. It was going to be up to Him to decide what was going to happen to them on Christmas Day. He'd ended up simply holding her in his arms while she leaned against him and dozed. Giving her comfort by simply being near.

Late into the night, several of his sisters had joined Amanda and Traci in the bedroom Joseph Vance had provided them. Dale had no idea if any of them had slept, but at least they had been able to provide them with some measure of support.

After refusing several offers of coffee or food when he walked by Joseph's large kitchen and dining room, Dale looked for Amanda. At last he found her sitting by herself in a small, secluded reading room. It was a beautiful room. The walls were made of dark paneled wood and the oak floors were covered in a thick oatmeal-colored rug. Two leather chairs and a love seat rested in the center of the room, all surrounding a roaring fire in a redbrick fireplace.

Amanda was curled up on the love seat. A small container of fabric and thread was by her side. She was staring into the fire, lost in thought.

He paused before entering the room. "Can I come in?"

"Oh! Of course." Resituating herself, she looked ready to spring to her feet. "Is . . . Is there any news?"

"No. I just was worried about you."

"Oh."

"What have you been doing? Have you been awake long?"

"I've been up maybe an hour. After getting a cup of coffee, Neil's uncle said I could sit in here. I told him that I needed to be someplace on my own for a while."

Instead of walking right in, he leaned against the doorway. He wanted her to feel free to tell him that she still did need to be alone. As much as he wanted to hold her close, he knew that her needs were what mattered most. "Looks like you've been working on a project."

"I wanted to finish this gift I've been making for Susanna." She held up a beautifully quilted pillowcase. It was a tulip pattern and was made of various patterns of pink, purple, turquoise, and blue fabrics.

"It's pretty." He smiled. "Bright."

She chuckled. "It is, indeed." She tilted her head to the side. "To be honest, these colors are not what Susanna usually leans towards. She may not care for it. But this is what I think of when I think of her."

He hated to seem dense, but he had no idea what she was talking about. "You think of Susanna in terms of pink and purple tulips?"

"*Nee*, silly. I think of her as light. She's bold and bright and steadfast. Those are the things I value in her."

Dale crossed the room and knelt by her side. After carefully moving the quilt out of her hands, he took them between his own. Then he spoke from his heart. "If she's those things to you, then they must be true. Wherever she is, whatever she is doing, she is going to survive and prevail. I am sure of it."

Flinging her arms around him, she pressed her face into his neck. "I hope so, Dale. I really do."

Next thing he knew, he moved his head and claimed her lips. With a sigh, she relaxed against him. Few things had ever felt so sweet.

All too soon, they heard a door open, then a lot of chatter.

Amanda broke away. "We should go see what happened."

Taking her hand in his, he led the way.

But what he saw happening in the front lawn took his breath away. Roy was speaking to his uncle, who looked as troubled as he did. Sheriff Brewer was standing about two feet away from them, speaking on his cell phone.

Amanda visibly steeled herself as they walked down the porch's front steps to hear what was going on. No one seemed to spare either of them a second look.

Instead, all the men who were there watched Sheriff Brewer disconnect his phone, signal to Deputy Beck, then walk over to Mr. and Mrs. Schwartz. "I think they're in the cave. There's an old boarded-up entrance on the outskirts of Horse Cave. Neil's mother had forgotten that she'd asked Neil and Susanna to deliver a gift out that way."

"We need to go there," Amanda's father said.

Sheriff Brewer nodded. "Deputy Beck is going to take you and your daughters there as soon as you are ready. I'm going to head there now with Roy and Joseph."

"So, we are close."

"I hope so, Mrs. Schwartz. Do you want to come, or would you rather wait here? I can give someone a cell phone and I can send word as soon as we have news."

"Definitely not. I want to be wherever my daughter is," she said. "You don't need to wait for me to get ready. I'm ready now."

Mr. Schwartz looked around the area. "Where is Neil's father?"

Sheriff Brewer exhaled. "He has been taken down to my office by another officer. I'm afraid we need him there for questioning."

Though Sheriff Brewer's voice was low, Dale felt as if every person in the whole front yard reeled in pain.

Suddenly, Roy's reluctance to speak to the authorities made complete sense.

CHAPTER 32

Monday, December 25

"Do you see that?" Neil said, pointing to a crack in the roof of the cave.

Wiping her eyes with what she hoped was a halfway-clean portion of her dress, Susanna raised her head to look where he was pointing. "See what?"

"Daylight," he said with a smile. "It's morning now. We made it through the night."

She blinked, her eyes and mind finally registering what she saw. Yes, indeed, there really was a narrow ray of light shining down upon them from up above.

After spending so many hours in the suffocating darkness, it felt as if the angels up in Heaven really had been listening to her fervent prayers.

"It's good to see, *jah?*"

Susanna turned to Neil, so glad that she could now actually see his face. A nasty-looking scrape was on his forehead. A dark bruise marred his right cheek. His eyes looked red and tired, and his hair was sticking up every which way. But his lips were now slightly curved in a smile as he watched her examine him.

"It is very good." She smiled back. "I don't think I'll ever take sunlight for granted again."

He chuckled. "Me, neither." Studying her, too, he said, "You look wonderful, Susanna."

"What? Surely not." Brushing a hand across her cheek, she attempted to smooth some of her hair back from her face. Her *kapp* had fallen off hours ago, as well as most of the pins securing her hair in place.

Still studying her, he said, "You are smiling. That makes you perfect."

Though his compliment was excessive, she knew what he meant. They could have been badly hurt last night. They could have lost hope, too. That would have been just as harmful, or maybe even worse. If they had given up, then they would have stopped trying to survive.

Shifting, she winced. Her body felt so stiff and sore. "I can't believe I fell asleep last night. The last thing I remember is talking to you about my mother's hospital stay."

He yawned. "I fell asleep, too. I didn't think it was possible, but it's good we did." Eyeing her hurt wrist, he said, "How is your arm feeling?"

Looking down at it, she shrugged. Her wrist was black and blue and looked at least double its normal size. "It hurts, but the cold air seems to help keep the pain under control."

"Maybe I could make a bandage for it out of your apron. Would you like me to try? I could rip the fabric into some strips. It might help."

She supposed it would, but for what end? There was nowhere for them to go. No place where she would be able to climb, even with two healthy arms. "Maybe in a little bit."

Some of his enthusiasm faded. "All right. Just, um, tell me when you are ready."

"I'll do that." Now, wishing she would have let him bandage her arm, if only to let him feel like he was doing something useful, she sighed.

Then, suddenly, she realized what day it was.

"Neil, guess what?"

"Hmm?"

"It's Christmas!"

"I guess it is." He smiled slightly. "Merry Christmas, Susanna."

"Merry Christmas to you."

They looked at each other. So much lay between them. Fear about being stuck in this cavern for days. Fear about never being found. Confusion about how they'd fallen into the cave in the first place.

Slowly, her smile faded away. And on its heels, tears threatened to return.

He noticed.

Scooting toward her, he shifted so he was leaning against the wall of the cavern. "Come here," he said, reaching out for her waist.

She was at first confused about what he wanted, but she followed his directives. Next thing she knew, she was sitting in between his stretched legs and leaning her back against his chest. He wrapped his arms around her middle, holding her close.

Immediately, warmth suffused her, relaxing her muscles

and enabling her to lean closer into him. "Your body is far more comfortable than hard limestone."

He chuckled. "Glad to know." Exhaling, he shifted so she was even more secured in his embrace. "This is better. Ain't so?"

She nodded. Behind her, she could feel his even breathing. She imagined that she could feel his heart beat as well. Its steady cadence calmed her like little else. She snuggled a bit closer to him, enjoying his comfort.

"I bet we will get rescued today."

"I hope so. I . . . I have a plan. If no one comes for us today, then tomorrow morning I'm going to have to find a way out."

"Neil, *nee*."

"It has to be done. You know that as well as I do."

"All right. But today you'll stay here?"

"Today, we can sit like this all day if you'd like."

She would like that. Not only did his arms around her feel warm and secure, she liked simply being so close to him. "I'm going to start praying even harder. I bet the Lord answers lots of prayers on Christmas Day."

"I imagine you're right. It's His son's birthday. A good time to grant wishes and prayers, I think."

Closing her eyes, Susanna prayed for strength and continued hope and for her family. She prayed for Sheriff Brewer and Deputy Beck and their efforts. She prayed for everyone who was no doubt tired and cold, walking outside looking for them.

"*The light shines in the darkness and the darkness has not overcome it*," she said aloud.

Neil lifted his chin. "What is that verse from? Matthew?"

"*Nee*. John. Do you remember how John speaks of light and darkness?"

After a moment, Neil said, *"The true light that enlightens every man was coming into the world."*

"I love that part," Susanna murmured. "It's fitting this morning, isn't it?"

She felt his chin lift. "Looking at our own little ray of light, I'd have to agree." After a pause, Neil said, "Sue, I need to tell you something."

"What is it?"

"I . . . I think it's my father who is behind everything."

"Behind the accidents?"

"Jah."

Everything inside her wanted to tell him that he was mistaken. No father would willingly trap his son in a cave. But she knew he wasn't speaking off the top of his head. "Why do you believe that?"

"A couple of things. He hasn't really recovered from the sale and the move. He blamed your family, himself, and my uncle."

She wasn't sure how that transferred to his father doing so much damage to a place that he claimed to love. Or, again, how he would go from breaking a fence to trapping the two of them in this cave. "He was really upset, I guess."

"He needed someone to blame. When it became obvious that no one was going to take his side any longer when he blamed your parents, he transferred most of the blame to my uncle Joseph."

"Well, the things you told me about your uncle do sound terrible."

"I thought so, too. At first."

"Did something change?"

"Yeah. I guess after meeting you and realizing just how much I misjudged your family, it got me wondering if I had

taken too much of what my father said at face value." He
paused. Clasped his hands together tightly before releasing
them. "I realized shortly after that the things he told me had
been tainted by his perception."

"Oh, Neil."

He released a ragged sigh. "I realized that when I sat alone
with Joseph. He said some things that made me think that he
wasn't the villain I had thought he would be."

"But why would your father do so many things to hurt my
family?"

"I don't think he thought anything through. It pains me to
say this, but I'm starting to realize that he doesn't think a lot of
things through. He is impulsive, I guess. Or, maybe more like
he has tunnel vision. At first, he wanted to keep that farm. He
wanted to do whatever he could to make that happen, even
making foolish choices and going further into debt. Then, instead of admitting his mistakes to me or Uncle Joseph, he sold
the land. But instead of taking responsibility for his actions, he
transferred all the blame to your parents. I think that's when
he decided you needed to leave the property."

"But even if we had left, it wouldn't have changed the situation. It still wouldn't have been your family's farm anymore."

"I know. It doesn't make any sense."

His voice was hoarse. Quiet and scratchy. It reminded her
a lot of how his voice sounded when she'd first heard him
after the accident. Filled with heavy emotion and regret, she
responded to it in a way she responded to few other things. It
made her yearn to help him and maybe to fight for herself. For
them.

Long moments passed. She could feel the tension emanating from his body. "What made you certain?" she finally asked.

"I wasn't sure until last night when I remembered my father and Uncle Joseph telling Roy and me stories about all the abandoned cave entrances. I realized that he would have known what this part of the cave was like. He would have known that we wouldn't likely have gotten too injured from our fall."

Susanna shivered. "But how could he know that for sure?"

"He didn't, of course. When I was trying to figure it all out, I remembered my mother telling him that you and I were going to deliver cookies. Everyone knows that no one goes to visit Velma. She's a recluse. She wouldn't have gone outside, and no one would have come by except for us."

"So he wanted us to fall?"

"I think he decided that it wasn't going to harm us. Just scare your family enough to make you move."

"I don't know what is going to happen to us now. But I do know that my family has been very afraid. So I guess he got his wish."

"I'm sorry, Susanna," he murmured, his voice thick with emotion. "I hope I'm wrong. I don't want to be right."

Startled, she realized his phrase was just what she'd said to him days ago, when she'd been so upset about not being believed. His apology made her ache for him. If he was right, how was he going to be able to bear that burden?

"There's no need for apologies. If you are right, if it was your father, it certainly wasn't your doing. And if you are wrong, well, that ain't your fault, either."

He didn't reply, only tightened his arms around her.

She felt his desolation. Realized that he was hurting. But she didn't seem to have any words for him. What could she say that could possibly ease his heart?

Instead, she relaxed against him. Showing him silently that

no matter what happened next she believed in him. Looking up at the glimmer of light, she tried to think of positive things. Tried to stay positive.

Eventually, she relaxed enough that her eyes drifted shut.

Only when a loud crack and clang erupted above her did she awake completely.

"Neil? Susanna?" After a pause, the voice rang through the cavern again. "Neil Vance! Susanna Schwartz! Can you hear me?"

"We're here!" Neil called out as he carefully slid away from her, then struggled to his feet. *"You found us!"*

Suddenly, Susanna was so overcome, she simply leaned back against the cave's wall. Leaned back against the place where Neil had been just moments before . . . and looked up at the bright opening above them.

Looking down was Deputy Beck, her father, and Roy Vance.

"Susanna!" her father said.

"Hiya, Daed," she said with a smile.

What had been lost had been found. And out of the darkness had come the light.

In all of its blinding goodness.

CHAPTER 33

Monday, December 25

I think it is still Christmas," Amanda said as she crept into
Susanna's room late that night.

Susanna glanced at the digital clock by her bedside. The
flashing numbers said it was a quarter after eleven. "We still
have forty-five minutes until it's over," she said, still not quite
sure if she was sad the day was over or relieved. Hands down,
it had been both the best and worst Christmas of her life.
"What are you doing here?"

Amanda stuffed one of her hands into a pocket of her
new robe, looking unsure. In her other, she held a flashlight.
"You're going to think this is silly, but I wanted to sleep in
here with you."

"Just like we used to."

"*Jah*. Do you mind?"

Susanna pulled the covers down on the other side of her
double bed. "Of course not. I couldn't sleep, either."

"Were you afraid of the dark? The doctors told Mamm

that you might need to sleep with a flashlight. I even brought us a second one in case you wanted it brighter."

She looked at the flashlight her father had set on her bedside table. She'd used it to get ready for bed, but had turned it off when she got under the covers. "*Nee.* I don't know why, but I'm not afraid. I was just thinking about Neil and Roy."

Amanda winced. "Knowing that their father had been taken in for questioning had to have been so awful for them. Devastating."

"*Jah.*"

"What do you think is going to happen to them all?"

"Based on how their uncle Joe wrapped his arms around Neil, I think they're going to heal. But first, they're going to have some difficult days ahead."

"Dale is really worried about all of them."

"I think everyone is." She knew she was. She'd felt like half the population of Horse Cave was standing outside the cave's entrance after firemen slid ladders down, secured them, then helped her and Neil climb up to safety.

The moment she'd gotten on solid ground and felt the sunlight on her face, she'd started crying. Her parents' and sisters' hugs had only made her cry harder.

Eventually, Deputy Beck had guided her to the ambulance. She'd sat on the tailgate and answered questions while Neil had hugged his mother fiercely, then learned that his father had already been taken to the sheriff's office.

Later, she'd taken a trip to the hospital for X-rays and tests. She'd left two hours after with a temporary cast on her arm and strict instructions to get plenty of rest for the next forty-eight hours.

"When do you think you'll see Neil again?"

"Tomorrow. He said he'd come over around noon."

"You two seem really close now."

"It would be hard not to be close after being stuck in the cave together," she said.

"Sue, I'm serious."

"I know. You're right. We . . . We are close. We said we loved each other," she shared softly.

"You did?" Pure wonder was in Amanda's voice. Hesitancy, too.

"*Jah.*" She held her breath, waiting for Amanda to comment about that. She wouldn't have blamed her for doubting Susanna's feelings toward Neil, either. A tumultuous event like that could make anyone say a lot of things they regretted in the morning light.

"I told Dale I loved him, too."

"Really?"

"*Jah.*" Sounding more like her confident self, she said, "Of course, he told me first. I think we are going to get engaged soon."

"What do you think Mamm is going to say?"

"She's probably going to ask for a long engagement. But the good news is that even if I do marry Dale sooner than later, we plan to live on his land. Both of us want to be close to our families."

"That's wonderful. Better than wonderful."

"I think so, too." Amanda rearranged the covers and slid down a couple more inches. "Do you need some more pain reliever or anything?"

"*Nee.* I'm good for now."

"Oh! Look at that," Amanda whispered.

Susanna turned her head and looked at the clock. It was now eleven fifty-eight. "I guess Christmas is just about over."

"You were my wish," Amanda said. "I prayed and prayed and prayed that you would come home. And you did."

"I was praying and praying that I would come home, too. It seems Jesus gave us our wishes on His birthday."

"Next year, we might each be married."

"Who knows what the year will bring?"

"We should make another Christmas wish," Amanda said. "Quickly. Before we run out of time."

"Amanda, I don't know if I can do one more thing today."

"Come on, this isn't hard. Hurry, now. Close your eyes and make a wish. It can't hurt."

Susanna couldn't find fault with that logic. So, therefore, she did as Amanda asked. She closed her eyes and let her heart and mind open. Wished Jesus a happy birthday and asked for one more gift . . . if it wasn't too much trouble.

She wished for peace.

Peace and love and hope and faith.

When she opened her eyes, she noticed a bright star out her window. Maybe it was Venus, maybe it was just a star.

But it was so bright it seemed to shine brighter than all the others. Making her darkness into something so bright, so luminous, that she knew Jesus had been listening, indeed.

For there, in her heart, lay only light.

"Merry Christmas, Susanna," Amanda mumbled sleepily beside her.

"Merry Christmas, sister," Susanna said. "And may God bless you. May God bless all of us."

About the author

About the book

Read on

Insights,
Interviews
& More . . .

Meet
Shelley Shepard Gray

In many ways, my writing journey has been like my faith journey. I entered into both with a lot of hope and a bit of nervousness. You see, I didn't get baptized until I was in my twenties and didn't first get published until I was in my thirties. Some people might consider those events to have happened a little late in life. However, I feel certain that God knew each took place at exactly the right time for me.

To be honest, these days I rarely stop to think about my life before I was a Christian or a writer. I simply wake up, drink my coffee, and try to get everything done that I can each day! I feel blessed to be a part of a large church family, to have my husband and children, and to enjoy a busy career. But

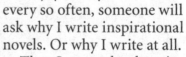

every so often, someone will ask why I write inspirational novels. Or why I write at all.

Then I remember how it felt to knock on a minister's office door and tell him that I wanted to be baptized; and how it felt the very first time I wrote "Chapter 1"—both felt exhilarating and nerve-wracking.

Perhaps you are a little bit like me. Maybe you, also, developed your faith a little after some of your friends or family. Maybe you, also,

The New Studio

began a new job in a field that you didn't go to school for. Maybe you started on a journey where you weren't sure you were going to be a success or even fit in.

Or maybe, like me, success wasn't what you were hoping to attain. Maybe it was a matter of following a power bigger than yourself. If so, I'm glad I'm in good company. I'd love to know your story, too.

Now I have been a Christian for almost thirty years. I've been a published writer for about half that time. Both journeys have not always been easy. Both have been filled with ups and downs. Yet, both have given me much joy, too. I'd like to think that anything worth having takes some hard work. It takes some time to grow and mature, too.

And because of that, I am comfortable with the fact that I'm still on my journey, one morning at a time.

With blessings to you,
Shelley Shepard Gray ∽

Letter from the Author

Last year's Christmas was really special! We had quite a houseful. Both of our kids were there. So was our new son-in-law, Alex. Tom's mom and his brother, Mike, came, too. And so did Dan and Suzanne.

There's a story about Dan. You see, we first met him when he was engaged to Betsy, who was Tom's sister. Over the years, we spent lots of holidays together. For some reason, Dan and I used to end up in the kitchen after the big meals. We'd wash dishes so the rest of the family could enjoy some time together. (Boy, did we wash a lot of dishes!) Then, several years ago, Betsy passed away. When the next holiday rolled around, we all missed her tremendously. But we missed Dan, too! It just didn't feel the same without either of them.

A couple of years ago, Dan met Suzanne and was gracious enough to invite all of us to their wedding. It was such a joyous occasion! Then, when it turned out that they were going to be near us for Christmas, Tom and I were thrilled to have them join us for the holidays once again. Actually, all of us were thrilled to have them join us. We all had a great time. We did the usual—ate too much, stayed up too late, and laughed a lot. We even washed dishes together! It was perfect.

I've thought about Dan and Suzanne a lot while writing this book. Maybe because so much of *The Gift* has to do with things that happened that were out of the characters' control.

The "gift" in this novel refers to a person who has been a particular blessing in my heroine's life. Maybe, like me, you can think of many people who fit this description.

If so, I hope you get to see them this holiday season. If not, maybe you'll get the chance to let them know how much they mean to you. That's a present worth giving, I think.

Merry Christmas!
Shelley ∽

Questions for Discussion

1. The inspiration for much of the novel came from 2 Corinthians, "We walk by faith, not by sight." What does this verse mean to you? When have you had to walk by faith?

2. I thought the Amish proverb— "Enjoy today. It won't come back"—had a lot of significance for a Christmas novel. I often find myself spending much of December counting down the days until Christmas Day instead of enjoying each moment of the season! Do you ever need to remind yourself to spend a little bit of time being grateful for each day, too?

3. What were your first impressions of Neil and Susanna? What about Dale and Amanda?

4. Have you moved to a new city or town before? What do you think is the hardest part? What blessings have happened because of a move?

5. I really enjoyed writing about Susanna, Amanda, and Traci's relationship. I enjoyed writing about three sisters who got along and wanted to support each other. Do you have such a relationship with one of your family members? How has that close bond helped you through the years?

6. My favorite scenes in the novel take place on Christmas Eve in the cavern. What were your favorite parts?

7. What is your favorite way to celebrate the Christmas season?

8. What relationships in your life have been an unexpected gift? How did the Lord lead you to these special people? ∽

Christmas Recipes for Gift Giving

(From *Our Family's Favorite Recipes*)

Apple Butter

2 qts. unsweetened applesauce
½ cup white sugar
½ cup brown sugar
⅓ tsp. allspice
1 tsp. cinnamon
⅓ tsp. cloves

Mix together. Can be put in an oven at 200 degrees or in a Crock-Pot uncovered. Simmer until thickened.

Caramel Corn

8 cups popcorn
¾ cup packed brown sugar
6 tbsps. margarine or butter
3 tbsps. light corn syrup
¼ tsp. salt
¼ tsp. baking soda
¼ tsp. vanilla extract

Put popcorn in baking dish. Measure sugar, butter, corn syrup, and salt into saucepan. Cook and stir until butter melts. Boil and cook for 3 minutes. Stir in soda and vanilla. Pour mixture over popcorn. Bake 15 minutes in 300-degree oven. Stir and bake 5 to 10 minutes longer. ∾

A Sneak Peek from the Next Book in the Amish of Hart County Series

Coming March 2018 from Avon Inspire!

SOMETIMES, THE SOUND of a phone ringing still caught Calvin Fisher off guard. When his cell buzzed for the second time, he pulled it out of his back pocket. Thumb hovering over the screen, he intended to press ignore, but then he noticed the area code.

Eight months ago, he promised he'd never ignore a call from Hart County again. As it buzzed a third time, the sound echoing through the dark alleyway, Calvin pressed answer.

"Hello?" he asked. "Mark, is that you?"

"Ack! *Nee*, Calvin. It's Waneta," his sister-in-law said in a rush. "Oh, Calvin. I'm so glad you answered."

"Me, too, Neeta," he murmured. "Hold on one sec, 'kay?" After motioning to the men nearby that he'd be right back, Calvin put the phone up to his ear and started walking. "You okay?" he asked, already feeling awkward. Of course Waneta wasn't okay if she was calling him. She was Amish and didn't get on the phone unless she had a good reason.

"I'm not okay at all. Oh, Calvin— Mark and me just got back from the *doktah*."

"What's wrong? Are you sick?"

"*Nee,* it's Mark, Calvin." She paused, her breath hitching something awful. "He's been feeling poorly for a while, you see, but he didn't want to let you know. Finally, he went to the *doktah* two days ago." She continued, hardly stopping for breath, each word bleeding into the next so fast that he had to stop walking in order to understand her better. "Dr. Hanna sent him to the hospital for tests, then he called us in to his office this morning."

"What did the doctor tell ya?" he asked as he unlocked the front door of the apartment complex where he lived and trotted up three flights of stairs.

"Th . . . That Mark has cancer."

A wave of dizziness hit him hard. He stopped again, gripping the worn metal banister so tightly that the edge of it cut into his palm.

"Calvin?" she asked hesitantly. "Calvin, are you still there?"

He closed his eyes. Waneta needed him. "I'm sorry, sis," he said, intentionally adding his new pet name for her in an effort to ease her worries. "I'm here. Um, what kind of cancer is it? Do you know?"

"It's renal cell something."

"Say again?"

"Oh, I can hardly pronounce it. I'm sorry, Calvin. It's something to do with his kidneys." Sounding more perturbed, she continued. "Dr. Hanna gave us some literature and a phone number of a nurse who can explain things *gut,* too. But I don't know. All I ▶

remember him saying is that Mark has cancer and is going to need to have one of his kidneys removed."

He'd finally made it to his apartment. Unlocking the door, he strode inside and bolted it firmly behind him. Then, as Waneta continued to talk about how worried she was, he did a quick walk-through, just to make sure no one had been in his place since he'd left six hours ago.

When he was assured that everything was undisturbed, he sat down on the chair in the corner of his darkened bedroom. Forced himself to remain calm and keep his voice steady. "Sis, where's Mark? Can I talk to him?"

"*Nee*. He's sleeping. Plus, I didn't tell him I was going to call you. This is Lora's phone."

"Okay. Is Lora there?" Lora was an old friend. They'd all grown up together. She, like Calvin, had left the Amish faith. But also like him, Lora hadn't wanted to remove her ties and live completely among the English. She'd married a local deputy in the sheriff's department. She had also become a close friend to all of them.

"Um, *jah*."

"Put her on the phone, Neeta," he said gently. As he heard the phone switch hands, he attempted to gather himself again. But really, all he felt was numb.

"Calvin?" Lora said at last. "Hey."

"Hey. Waneta told me about Mark's

diagnosis. Have you seen the paperwork? Did you talk to Mark?"

"I talked to both of them. The doctor is very sure, Calvin. Mark has, um, renal cell carcinoma in his right kidney. They want to schedule an operation as soon as possible. Like next week. Can you be there?"

"Of course." Making the decision, he got to his feet. "I'll leave tomorrow morning."

"Thanks." Lowering her voice, she said, "Mark and Neeta are going to need your help."

"That's good because I want to help. Tell Waneta that I'll see her in the early afternoon."

"I'll do that." He heard Lora murmur something to Waneta as they seemed to move into another room. "Calvin, I need to ask . . . Are you going to bring trouble here?"

He knew what she was asking. As far as she, Mark, Waneta, and the rest of the world knew, he was still involved in a gang. He still did a lot of things that were illegal and that brought on trouble of one kind or another.

"Hope not," he said, purposely keeping his tone light as he strode into the kitchen to get a glass of water.

"You hope not?" Her voice rose. "Calvin, if your being here is going to bring your gun-toting, drug-running friends here, then you need to stay away. Actually, you should tell—"

He cut her off. "Gun-toting, drug- ▶

A Sneak Peek *(continued)*

running friends?" he said with a forced laugh. "You make me sound like some kind of gangster. Have you been watching old movies on TV again?"

"Don't joke about this," she replied in a steely voice. "You might be pretending that I'm as naïve as half the population of Munfordville, Kentucky, but we both know that ain't me. I'm serious. You can't bring your problems and bad habits to your brother's doorstep."

As he filled his glass with water from the tap, he found himself wishing again that he could tell someone, anyone, what he was really up to. But because that wasn't possible, he kept his reply light. "Nothing's going to happen. Settle down before you get Waneta riled up. Everything is going to be fine." Before she could go off on him again, he decided it was time to end the call. "Don't forget to remind Neeta that I'll be there tomorrow. Bye."

Calvin hung up before Lora could reply or give him another warning. After tossing his phone on the counter, he drained his glass, then filled it up again.

When he slowly set the glass back on the counter, he smiled to himself. Yeah, that's what he was drinking now when he got stressed out. Tap water. He wasn't sure if Lora would have been more shocked or relieved to see that he was no longer enjoying shots of tequila or a six-pack of beer when things got stressful. It hadn't been easy, but he had cleaned himself up.

Well, at least in private.

Out in public, though? That was a different story. His reputation depended on him being filled with vices and excuses.

When his phone buzzed again, followed by two heavy raps on his door, Calvin carefully set the glass in the sink, grabbed his phone, and approached the door.

He took a minute to get his head back where it needed to be. He couldn't show weakness. He couldn't allow anyone to see an inkling of fear or worry or strain in his eyes. After standing up straighter, he exhaled, then pulled open the door. "What?"

"Boss wants you, Cal," Jenk, one of the men he'd been standing in the alley with, said. Stepping closer, he peered into his apartment. "What's going on? You sure took off quick when you got that phone call." Grinning, he said, "You got someone in here or something? One of your old Amish buddies?"

"If I did, it ain't none of your business, right?" The gang knew he'd been born Amish but believed he had been shunned by his family and had cut all ties with everyone else.

Jenk shrank back, stung. "No. 'Course not." Now looking at him warily, he shifted his feet. "So, you coming or what?"

Instead of answering, Calvin pulled out his keys and locked his door. He kept his chin up and his expression blank as he walked with Jenk down the hallway. By the time he was walking down the ▶

stairs, he was no longer thinking about his brother or Hart County or cancer. Instead, all he cared about was the reassuring weight of the pistol nestled against the small of his back and the fact that no one else was loitering in the area wanting to talk to him.

When they finally stepped outside, his transformation was complete. To everyone in Louisville, he wasn't Calvin, the former Amish younger brother of Mark Fisher. Instead, he was Cal, the former homeless loser who had found a home with one of the strongest drug-running gangs in the state of Kentucky.

He was also an undercover informant for the DEA.

And he now had less than twenty-four hours to make up a reason to leave that was believable enough to keep everything that he did in this place very far from Horse Cave.

Otherwise, he wouldn't only be bringing his trouble to his brother's house. He'd be bringing danger to everyone there, too. ❧